MODERN RETIREMENT PLANNING

WHAT YOU DON'T KNOW CAN COST YOU EVERYTHING!

David A. Kutcher, CLTC and Richard C. Scott, CLU, LUTCF

ABOUT THE AUTHOR

Dave is a graduate of Bridgewater State College and spent 15 years as a ground combat infantry officer in the Marine Corps. Dave has dedicated his time and resources to helping people understand and become an active voice in their own retirement income planning. Dave is active in his community, lives in Wasilla, Alaska with his wife, Vanessa, three kids and four dogs and is an avid outdoorsman who enjoys spending his spare time in the woods and on the water. With over 30 years of experience, Dave, an independent financial professional, prides himself on his ability to locate products and offer services that drive people toward their financial objectives. Educating his clients about the different options available to them is important to Dave, and his goal is to simplify complex issues of retirement for clients planning for their futures.

ABOUT THE AUTHOR

Rick has been in the financial services business since 1983, serving in a multitude of positions, with the last 15+ years focused on advanced case design in both the estate and business planning markets, where he has earned a reputation for excellence in all that he does. Rick's lifelong dedication to the business has resulted in his achievement of numerous industry awards, both for his service to clients as well as his service to the business itself. He has served in many leadership roles in industry associations. Rick prides himself on his ability to find and implement viable solutions for his clients' journeys to and through retirement. Rick's formal education in finance is from Boston University, but he insists the best lessons in his career have come from dedicated and thorough work in helping clients reach their goals and objectives. Rick and his family reside on a small ranch in a rural, northwestern section of Rhode Island where horses, cattle, sheep, and goats are around every turn. He thoroughly enjoys having served as a youth hockey coach for the past 14 years and enjoys all things outdoors.

MODERN RETIREMENT PLANNING

WHAT YOU DON'T KNOW CAN COST YOU EVERYTHING!

Dave and Rick, Ted Stevens International Airport, Anchorage, AK 2023

David A. Kutcher, CLTC and Richard C. Scott, CLU, LUTCF

Book Designed and Published by Aeyshaa
@ Ryterly Publishing

TABLE OF CONTENTS

INTRODUCTION

In 2011 Dave was the owner and was active in a business in New Hampshire called DAK Financial Group. Rick, as owner of North East Insurance Planning, Inc, was managing the New England territory for an insurance company, recruiting new producers and providing sales support primarily in the form of case design. The two hit it off from the moment they met and continued to forge a productive and rewarding business relationship.

As time went by, Dave and Rick continued to find ways to work together even as they each made separate and distinct changes to their respective overall business plans. They recognize that each of them brings something different in terms of value in working together and it became obvious that their skillsets complemented each other in a way that would support a mutually beneficial business relationship with lots of synergy.

Starting with some baby steps, they formed a partnership with defined roles and soon thereafter proceeded to create a new entity with common ownership, known today as Frontier Retirement, Inc.

Dave and Rick bring years of experience to the financial considerations required to create and maintain an efficient and beneficial retirement strategy. Each has honed their respective skills and knowledge and, together, they provide a unique and conscientious approach to retirement planning.

They each truly consider their role in working with clients as one responsible for providing expert guidance and they rely on their years of real-life experiences in the financial services business as their own guide to helping folks make good decisions for themselves. Their perspective focuses on things that are truly impactful for retirement plan design. They believe their perspective is key to making sure current retirees, as well as those now approaching the precipice of retirement, have the knowledge and tools available to them to make informed decisions. Dave and Rick are guided by their self-titled motto of *"Safety, Growth and Control"* for their clients.

Their business model includes strategic relationships with other trusted advisors in the many specialties applicable to retirees and their respective planning needs. Neither Frontier Retirement, Inc. nor David and Rick individually receive any compensation from these working relationships. These include but are not limited to elder planning and estate planning attorneys, Medicare supplement specialists, and registered investment advisors.

Retirement Planning requires very different thinking and planning in terms of financial strategy than that which you employed during the years of accumulating assets for retirement. The strategies used to accumulate your retirement nest egg shift to strategies that are focused on deploying assets over your remaining lifetime while also positioning yourself to mitigate and/or minimize the impact of the many roadblocks that can come your way. There are risks during the time leading up to retirement, when you are focused on accumulating money, as well as during the time you are retiring. The risks during the latter of these two distinct phases of your life, however, come with a stark realization that time is not your friend and you no longer have the luxury of being able to make up for losses since you won't be working and generating outside income. Substantive financial events can be far more impactful at retirement than they were when you were younger. Good preparation is key and properly positioning yourself to handle the financial risks ahead will afford you the best opportunity to succeed in your retirement years and lead into your final financial phase of your life, your financial legacy.

Retirement is meant to be rewarding for you. They're not called "The Golden Years" for nothing. You have worked your entire life for this...take the time and energy it requires to be as well informed as you can be and establish plans that provide some certainty in the years ahead while providing adequate income to meet your objectives and yet keep you positioned to weather whatever storm may come your way.

PROLOGUE

Building a successful retirement plan is a common objective for most people, and even with the plethora of information that is available today, the ever-present challenges and risks associated with achieving a plan that is sustainable and viable leaves much uncertainty around some very basic, but extremely important questions. The answers to these questions, if we can solve them, will help determine if we are on track for success when we arrive on the doorstep of retirement.

◊ How much money (capital) do you need to accumulate by the time you retire? "The Nest Egg"

◊ How much net after-tax *income* do you and your family need, not just to meet basic living expenses, but also to enjoy the fruits of your lifelong labor while at the same time keeping pace with inflation and accounting for significant unexpected financial events?

◊ How long will you and your spouse or other loved ones need income? Longevity planning is key to making sure that you do not run out of money before your demise.

There are many other questions to consider too. In the following chapters we will ideally help you get started to find the answers to these important questions. At the very least, we hope you will see value in working together with a financial sherpa to help you consider the things we see as vital for you to understand. Again, this time in your financial life requires different thinking than you're used to. Achieving the highest rate of return on your money is not the primary goal as it was while you were accumulating money. There is as much, if not more, that needs consideration during the years ahead for you and your family.

The approach to Retirement Planning seems to fall into two primary, philosophical categories for those of us working in the financial services business; one where excess returns are sought and thought to be the remedy for all other risks that we will face during retirement, and those of us who employ a more broad use of financial products that we believe can provide a more certain outcome for you without sacrificing lifestyle. We believe that in real life there is significant value to certainty, and we believe "peace of mind" is undervalued in general in the planning process as you look to navigate what may potentially be 25-30 more years of your life.

After years of experience in this field, we feel strongly that our clients are better served by adopting an approach that provides more certainty and mitigates risk in ways that do *not* rely solely on better than average rates of return. In fact, many people are not in the financial position necessary to carry the risk that is associated with seeking the extraordinary returns that would be required to cover the types of major expenses that are often on the road ahead. The higher the risk, the higher the volatility tends to be, and volatility can create major headaches when there is a systematic distribution of income that is desired-or worse yet, required to meet IRS regulations.

As you are exposed to various ideas and terms in the chapters ahead, we ask that you try and stay focused on what a solution does, not what it is. Many people have preconceived notions about certain financial vehicles/products and that can lead to missed opportunities in seeking the most efficient and rewarding solutions to meet your specific needs. Financial products have changed significantly over the years and what your parents or grandparents may have had available to them is likely far different than what is available today...don't close your mind to financial solutions based upon outdated conceptions of what certain products provide for benefits.

We have done our best to be sure the charts and graphs included herein are accurate. None of the examples of product solutions represent any particular company. Examples are for illustrative purposes only and are provided to help clarify what is being presented. Our clients are always provided with proper disclosure regarding specific recommendations at the appropriate time.

We have written this book for the layperson, not for financial professionals. We have formed our opinions and comport ourselves today based upon the influence and knowledge passed on to us from others in this business who are much smarter than we are, as well as from our own observations in working with thousands of clients over the years. There are simply too many of those business associates along the way to name everyone individually-but we certainly appreciate all that we have learned from others.

Speaking of influence and related to this book specifically, Rick would be the first to tell you that many of the ideas on the pages ahead are rooted in ideas presented to him several years ago by a Managing Partner of a financial planning firm in Boston, MA who introduced Rick to the ideas and analysis of a man named Wade Pfau, Ph.D., CFA, RICP. The knowledge, commitment to fair analysis and attention to detail that is evident in Pfau's work is illustrated in a far more thorough presentation called "The Retirement Researchers Guide Series" book, *Safety-First Retirement Planning, An Integrated Approach for a Worry-Free Retirement.*

David has worked almost exclusively in the retirement planning marketplace demographic, and he has learned to listen and discern what really matters for folks who are approaching or already in their retirement years. He has shaped his ideas and finds his motivation in making certain that people he works with find solutions that truly matter in people's lives. Net, spendable income is the goal coupled with risk mitigation strategies. You can hear David every week in our radio address, by the way, and you can learn a little more about us, including access to some prior TV show recordings by visiting us at www.frontierretirement.com

David is on the air every Saturday morning from 8:30 am to 9:30 am Alaska time on KENI radio and Tuesday's and Thursday's from 8:00 am to 9:00 am on KBYR, station 700.

Together, Dave and Rick rely on their years of real-life experience working with real people, where emotional and psychological factors are worthy of consideration…as previously mentioned, "Peace of Mind" is particularly valuable and consequential during this time of your life and while something may appear on paper as a better choice or solution, something else may provide far more certainty and thus, Peace of Mind, affording you, as a retiree, a chance to better enjoy your day to day life without worry in the years ahead. Coincidentally, we have found that when someone has peace of mind and some inherent certainty built into their plans, even though they *may* sacrifice some rate of return on their retirement funds, they are likely to be willing to enjoy more of their retirement income potential because they know if the train derails, they have plans in place to help mitigate that event.

"Safety, Growth and Control"

Before we get into too much more, we thought we would take this opportunity to provide just one simple example of how taking action to provide some certainty for covering unknown events during retirement can give you the leeway to expand your choices as you look to provide a sustainable and more worry-free retirement experience.

What we want you to see in the following three exhibits is that by incorporating alternative financial resources that are available to you today, even if that means allocating these resources away from income production, we can actually produce a more certain and sustainable outlook for the later years of your retirement and ultimately provide you with more spendable income without sacrificing your legacy at your demise.

We are going to look at two scenarios in Exhibits 1-3. We are comparing an uninsured plan of action and an insured plan of action regarding potential Long Term Care expenses in the future.

On the left-hand side, the uninsured plan begins with a $2,000,000 nest egg and relies solely on the account values of the portfolio to fund both income needs as well as a future Long Term Care (LTC) event. On the right-hand side, we have carved out $200,000 (10%) of the available funds and deposited that $200,000 in a Hybrid Long Term Care Annuity. This annuity product provides leverage for a pool of LTC benefits initially equal to 3 X the premium deposit and the values inside the policy earn current interest rates less a small expense for the LTC coverage component with any net earnings increasing all three components of the policy; cash value, death benefit and LTC pool of benefits.

More specifically, we are comparing several choices you might have in using such a strategy…

- ◊ Take the *same percentage of income from both sides* of the equation - what does that result in for the total portfolio after a LTC event 12 years from now.
- ◊ Take *larger increases to income each year from the insured account* to level the total income over the period shown on both sides of the equation…in other words, what if you wanted to be sure not to sacrifice any income distribution even though you want the LTC protection.
- ◊ Take *more income on the insured plan and enjoy more spendable income* knowing that you don't have to be so concerned with a potential LTC event since you have it covered.

Here are the assumptions for you to know when looking at Exhibits 1-3.

- ◊ Assumed level rate of return on investment portfolio: 7%
- ◊ Exhibit 1-3 assumes a 3% *distribution* rate for both sides of the comparison.
- ◊ Annual *increases* in the income being distributed are 3% in Exhibit 1, 4% in Exhibit 2 and 5.25% in Exhibit 3.

◊ LTC plan: A hybrid product that provides leverage on the premium deposited equal to 3 X the amount of the deposit. So, a $200,000 deposit produces a potential LTC pool of benefits equal to $600,000. In this example, both spouses can share the pool of benefits if needed.

Exhibit 1.

Investment Account	$ 2,000,000			
	A	B	C	D
Year	Annual Withdrawal 3% / 3 % CPI	Remaining Portfolio Balance Assumes 7% No LTC EVENT	Long Term Care Event Expense	Remaining Portfolio Balance Assumes 7% AFTER LTC EVENT
1	$ 60,000	$ 2,075,800		$ 2,075,800
2	$ 61,800	$ 2,154,980		$ 2,154,980
3	$ 63,654	$ 2,237,719		$ 2,237,719
4	$ 65,564	$ 2,324,206		$ 2,324,206
5	$ 67,531	$ 2,414,643		$ 2,414,643
6	$ 69,556	$ 2,509,242		$ 2,509,242
7	$ 71,643	$ 2,608,231		$ 2,608,231
8	$ 73,792	$ 2,711,850		$ 2,711,850
9	$ 76,006	$ 2,820,352		$ 2,820,352
10	$ 78,286	$ 2,934,011		$ 2,934,011
11	$ 80,635	$ 3,053,112		$ 3,053,112
12	$ 83,054	$ 3,177,962	$ (250,000)	$ 2,910,462
13	$ 85,546	$ 3,308,885	$ (250,000)	$ 2,755,160
14	$ 88,112	$ 3,446,227	$ (100,000)	$ 2,746,742
15	$ 90,755	$ 3,590,355		$ 2,841,905
16	$ 93,478	$ 3,741,659		$ 2,940,817
17	$ 96,282	$ 3,900,552		$ 3,043,652
18	$ 99,171	$ 4,067,478		$ 3,150,595
19	$ 102,146	$ 4,242,906		$ 3,261,841
20	$ 105,210	$ 4,427,334		$ 3,377,594
Total:	$ 1,612,222		$ (600,000)	
Variance:				

Investment Account / HYBRID LTC ANNUITY	$ 1,800,000 / $200,000						
	E	F	G	H	I	J	K
Year	Annual Withdrawal 3% / 3% CPI	Remaining Portfolio Assumes 7% No LTC EVENT	Annuity Cash Value Assumes Current Rates	Total Balance Remaining NO LTC EVENT	Long Term Care Event Expense	Long Term Care Benefits $600,000	Remaining Total Balance After LTC EVENT
1	$ 54,000	$ 1,868,220	$ 194,683	$ 2,062,903		$ 629,619	$ 2,062,903
2	$ 55,620	$ 1,939,482	$ 194,762	$ 2,134,244		$ 660,699	$ 2,134,244
3	$ 57,289	$ 2,013,947	$ 196,651	$ 2,210,598		$ 693,314	$ 2,210,598
4	$ 59,007	$ 2,091,785	$ 198,540	$ 2,290,325		$ 727,540	$ 2,290,325
5	$ 60,777	$ 2,173,179	$ 200,429	$ 2,373,608		$ 763,454	$ 2,373,608
6	$ 62,601	$ 2,258,318	$ 202,317	$ 2,460,635		$ 801,142	$ 2,460,635
7	$ 64,479	$ 2,347,408	$ 204,206	$ 2,551,614		$ 840,689	$ 2,551,614
8	$ 66,413	$ 2,440,665	$ 206,095	$ 2,646,760		$ 882,190	$ 2,646,760
9	$ 68,406	$ 2,538,317	$ 207,984	$ 2,746,301		$ 925,738	$ 2,746,301
10	$ 70,458	$ 2,640,610	$ 212,806	$ 2,853,416		$ 971,437	$ 2,853,416
11	$ 72,571	$ 2,747,801	$ 218,973	$ 2,966,774		$1,019,391	$ 2,966,774
12	$ 74,749	$ 2,860,166	$ 225,324	$ 3,085,490	$ (250,000)	$ 819,713	$ 2,835,490
13	$ 76,991	$ 2,977,997	$ 231,866	$ 3,209,863	$ (250,000)	$ 603,896	$ 2,951,594
14	$ 79,301	$ 3,101,605	$ 238,604	$ 3,340,209	$ (100,000)	$ 534,130	$ 3,073,353
15	$ 81,680	$ 3,231,320	$ 245,545	$ 3,476,865		$ 566,177	$ 3,201,090
16	$ 84,130	$ 3,367,493	$ 252,693	$ 3,620,186		$ 600,148	$ 3,335,147
17	$ 86,654	$ 3,510,497	$ 260,056	$ 3,770,553		$ 636,157	$ 3,475,888
18	$ 89,254	$ 3,660,730	$ 267,640	$ 3,928,370		$ 674,326	$ 3,623,698
19	$ 91,931	$ 3,818,615	$ 275,452	$ 4,094,067		$ 714,786	$ 3,778,991
20	$ 94,689	$ 3,984,601	$ 283,497	$ 4,268,098		$ 757,673	$ 3,942,203
Total:	$ 1,451,000				$ (600,000)		
	$ (161,222) A-E						$ 564,608 K-D

On the left-hand side of the chart above you will see that we started with a $2,000,000 investment portfolio and on the right-hand side, we are starting with $1,800,000 since we are allocating $200,000 of our available funds to a hybrid LTC product.

- ◊ Columns A and E reflect a 3% annual distribution rate from the investment portfolio and the amount is indexed each year going forward to accommodate a 3% CPI based inflation adjustment
- ◊ Columns B and F reflect the *investment portfolio* only balance assuming there is NO LTC event that occurs. Column H includes the cash values inside the LTC Annuity on top of the smaller investment account.
- ◊ The first thing we want you to see regarding the insured side of the equation is that while there *was* $161,222 less total income provided to the retiree over the 20-year period in this particular example, the ending balance of available funds is $564,608 higher at the end of 20 years, as is reflected at the bottom of column K.

Exhibit 2

Investment Account	$ 2,000,000			
	A	B	C	D
Year	Annual Withdrawal 3% / 3 % CPI	Remaining Portfolio Balance Assumes 7% No LTC EVENT	Long Term Care Event Expense	Remaining Portfolio Balance Assumes 7% AFTER LTC EVENT
1	$ 60,000	$ 2,075,800		$ 2,075,800
2	$ 61,800	$ 2,154,980		$ 2,154,980
3	$ 63,654	$ 2,237,719		$ 2,237,719
4	$ 65,564	$ 2,324,206		$ 2,324,206
5	$ 67,531	$ 2,414,643		$ 2,414,643
6	$ 69,556	$ 2,509,242		$ 2,509,242
7	$ 71,643	$ 2,608,231		$ 2,608,231
8	$ 73,792	$ 2,711,850		$ 2,711,850
9	$ 76,006	$ 2,820,352		$ 2,820,352
10	$ 78,286	$ 2,934,011		$ 2,934,011
11	$ 80,635	$ 3,053,112		$ 3,053,112
12	$ 83,054	$ 3,177,962	$ (250,000)	$ 2,910,462
13	$ 85,546	$ 3,308,885	$ (250,000)	$ 2,755,160
14	$ 88,112	$ 3,446,227	$ (100,000)	$ 2,746,742
15	$ 90,755	$ 3,590,355		$ 2,841,905
16	$ 93,478	$ 3,741,659		$ 2,940,817
17	$ 96,282	$ 3,900,552		$ 3,043,652
18	$ 99,171	$ 4,067,478		$ 3,150,595
19	$ 102,146	$ 4,242,906		$ 3,261,841
20	$ 105,210	$ 4,427,334		$ 3,377,594
Total:	$ 1,612,222		$ (600,000)	
Variance:				

Investment Account	$ 1,800,000						
HYBRID LTC ANNUITY	$200,000						
	E	F	G	H	I	J	K
Year	Annual Withdrawal 3% / 4% CPI	Remaining Portfolio Assumes 7% No LTC EVENT	Annuity Cash Value Assumes Current Rates	Total Balance Remaining NO LTC EVENT	Long Term Care Event Expense	Long Term Care Benefits $600,000	Remaining Total Balance After LTC EVENT
1	$ 54,000	$ 1,868,220	$ 194,683	$ 2,062,903		$ 629,619	$ 2,062,903
2	$ 56,160	$ 1,938,904	$ 194,762	$ 2,133,666		$ 660,699	$ 2,133,666
3	$ 58,406	$ 2,012,133	$ 196,651	$ 2,208,784		$ 693,314	$ 2,208,784
4	$ 60,743	$ 2,087,987	$ 198,540	$ 2,286,527		$ 727,540	$ 2,286,527
5	$ 63,172	$ 2,166,552	$ 200,429	$ 2,366,981		$ 763,454	$ 2,366,981
6	$ 65,699	$ 2,247,912	$ 202,317	$ 2,450,229		$ 801,142	$ 2,450,229
7	$ 68,327	$ 2,332,156	$ 204,206	$ 2,536,362		$ 840,689	$ 2,536,362
8	$ 71,060	$ 2,419,373	$ 206,095	$ 2,625,468		$ 882,190	$ 2,625,468
9	$ 73,903	$ 2,509,653	$ 207,984	$ 2,717,637		$ 925,738	$ 2,717,637
10	$ 76,859	$ 2,603,089	$ 212,806	$ 2,815,895		$ 971,437	$ 2,815,895
11	$ 79,933	$ 2,699,777	$ 218,973	$ 2,918,750		$ 1,019,391	$ 2,918,750
12	$ 83,131	$ 2,799,812	$ 225,324	$ 3,025,136	$ (250,000)	$ 819,713	$ 2,775,136
13	$ 86,456	$ 2,903,291	$ 231,866	$ 3,135,157	$ (250,000)	$ 603,896	$ 2,876,888
14	$ 89,914	$ 3,010,314	$ 238,604	$ 3,248,918	$ (100,000)	$ 534,130	$ 2,982,062
15	$ 93,511	$ 3,120,979	$ 245,545	$ 3,366,524		$ 566,177	$ 3,090,750
16	$ 97,251	$ 3,235,389	$ 252,693	$ 3,488,082		$ 600,148	$ 3,203,044
17	$ 101,141	$ 3,353,646	$ 260,056	$ 3,613,702		$ 636,157	$ 3,319,036
18	$ 105,187	$ 3,475,851	$ 267,640	$ 3,743,491		$ 674,326	$ 3,438,819
19	$ 109,394	$ 3,602,109	$ 275,452	$ 3,877,561		$ 714,786	$ 3,562,485
20	$ 113,770	$ 3,732,523	$ 283,497	$ 4,016,020		$ 757,673	$ 3,690,125
Total:	$ 1,608,016				$ (600,000)		
	$ (4,206)						$ 312,531
	A-E						K-D

In exhibit 2, we have adjusted the income in the LTC covered situation so that it more closely matches the total income provided over the twenty years as compared to the portfolio that isn't covered for an LTC event.

◊ Each strategy provides virtually the same total income over the 20-year period. On the left-hand side we are sticking to the original 3% distribution rate from $2,000,000 and on the right-hand side, because we have more certainty about a potential LTC event, we feel safer distributing a slightly higher *increase* in income each year moving forward -In this example, we are distributing a 4% increase each year resulting in almost the same exact income being paid out over the 20 year period.

◊ Not only were we able to provide essentially the same income over the period shown, we did so while we also mitigating a $600,000 LTC expense and even still we had $312,531 more funds available at the end of the 20-year period.

Exhibit 3.

Investment Account	$ 2,000,000			
	A	B	C	D
Year	Annual Withdrawal 3% / 3 % CPI	Remaining Portfolio Balance Assumes 7% No LTC EVENT	Long Term Care Event Expense	Remaining Portfolio Balance Assumes 7% AFTER LTC EVENT
1	$ 60,000	$ 2,075,800		$ 2,075,800
2	$ 61,800	$ 2,154,980		$ 2,154,980
3	$ 63,654	$ 2,237,719		$ 2,237,719
4	$ 65,564	$ 2,324,206		$ 2,324,206
5	$ 67,531	$ 2,414,643		$ 2,414,643
6	$ 69,556	$ 2,509,242		$ 2,509,242
7	$ 71,643	$ 2,608,231		$ 2,608,231
8	$ 73,792	$ 2,711,850		$ 2,711,850
9	$ 76,006	$ 2,820,352		$ 2,820,352
10	$ 78,286	$ 2,934,011		$ 2,934,011
11	$ 80,635	$ 3,053,112		$ 3,053,112
12	$ 83,054	$ 3,177,962	$ (250,000)	$ 2,910,462
13	$ 85,546	$ 3,308,885	$ (250,000)	$ 2,755,160
14	$ 88,112	$ 3,446,227	$ (100,000)	$ 2,746,742
15	$ 90,755	$ 3,590,355		$ 2,841,905
16	$ 93,478	$ 3,741,659		$ 2,940,817
17	$ 96,282	$ 3,900,552		$ 3,043,652
18	$ 99,171	$ 4,067,478		$ 3,150,595
19	$ 102,146	$ 4,242,906		$ 3,261,841
20	$ 105,210	$ 4,427,334		$ 3,377,594
Total:	$ 1,612,222		$ (600,000)	
Variance:				

Investment Account / HYBRID LTC ANNUITY	$ 1,800,000 / $200,000						
	E	F	G	H	I	J	K
Year	Annual Withdrawal 3% / 5.25% CPI	Remaining Portfolio Assumes 7% No LTC EVENT	Annuity Cash Value Assumes Current Rates	Total Balance Remaining NO LTC EVENT	Long Term Care Event Expense	Long Term Care Benefits $600,000	Remaining Total Balance After LTC EVENT
1	$ 54,000	$ 1,868,220	$ 194,683	$ 2,062,903		$ 629,619	$ 2,062,903
2	$ 56,835	$ 1,938,182	$ 194,762	$ 2,132,944		$ 660,699	$ 2,132,944
3	$ 59,819	$ 2,009,849	$ 196,651	$ 2,206,500		$ 693,314	$ 2,206,500
4	$ 62,959	$ 2,083,171	$ 198,540	$ 2,281,711		$ 727,540	$ 2,281,711
5	$ 66,265	$ 2,158,090	$ 200,429	$ 2,358,519		$ 763,454	$ 2,358,519
6	$ 69,744	$ 2,234,531	$ 202,317	$ 2,436,848		$ 801,142	$ 2,436,848
7	$ 73,405	$ 2,312,405	$ 204,206	$ 2,516,611		$ 840,689	$ 2,516,611
8	$ 77,259	$ 2,391,606	$ 206,095	$ 2,597,701		$ 882,190	$ 2,597,701
9	$ 81,315	$ 2,472,011	$ 207,984	$ 2,679,995		$ 925,738	$ 2,679,995
10	$ 85,584	$ 2,553,477	$ 212,806	$ 2,766,283		$ 971,437	$ 2,766,283
11	$ 90,077	$ 2,635,838	$ 218,973	$ 2,854,811		$ 1,019,391	$ 2,854,811
12	$ 94,806	$ 2,718,904	$ 225,324	$ 2,944,228	$ (250,000)	$ 819,713	$ 2,694,228
13	$ 99,784	$ 2,802,459	$ 231,866	$ 3,034,325	$ (250,000)	$ 603,896	$ 2,776,055
14	$ 105,022	$ 2,886,257	$ 238,604	$ 3,124,861	$ (100,000)	$ 534,130	$ 2,858,006
15	$ 110,536	$ 2,970,022	$ 245,545	$ 3,215,567		$ 566,177	$ 2,939,793
16	$ 116,339	$ 3,053,441	$ 252,693	$ 3,306,134		$ 600,148	$ 3,021,095
17	$ 122,447	$ 3,136,163	$ 260,056	$ 3,396,219		$ 636,157	$ 3,101,554
18	$ 128,875	$ 3,217,798	$ 267,640	$ 3,485,438		$ 674,326	$ 3,180,766
19	$ 135,641	$ 3,297,908	$ 275,452	$ 3,573,360		$ 714,786	$ 3,258,284
20	$ 142,762	$ 3,376,006	$ 283,497	$ 3,659,503		$ 757,673	$ 3,333,608
Total:	$ 1,833,474				$ (600,000)		
	$ 221,252 (A-E)						$ (43,986) (K-D)

In Exhibit 3 you can see you are able to draw significantly more income in an attempt to maximize your annual increases to income, while still protecting yourself from an LTC event and not compromising on your total remaining funds at the end of the 20-year period.

◊ Column E now reflects a 5.25% increase each year on the income distribution vs. 4% in the prior example and vs. 3% in the original example.

◊ With only a small difference in ending values projected between columns K and D, you were able to distribute $221,252 more income to yourself over the first 20 years of your retirement and fully cover the $600,000 LTC expense. That is equivalent to approximately $10,000 more income per year.

What did we learn or confirm here?

1. Allocating resources for unknown future financial events can provide some certainty to your concerns for the years ahead and do so without compromising on income distribution needs over time.

2. When incorporating certain risk management features into our overall plan, you can make choices as to how you want to have those decisions impact various components of your overall financial picture...do you need to equate income of an insured plan to one that is self-insured? Or would you rather take a little less income now and keep the principal balance of your funds ahead of where they would be otherwise? Incorporating properly designed insurance based financial products provides peace of mind and certainty to an overall plan and peace of mind has value in your golden years.

Certainty

Certainty is the state of being sure or confident about something, or something that is very likely to happen.

Certainty profoundly shapes our behavior. The more certain we are of a belief—regardless of its objective correctness—the more durable it will be and the greater its influence on what we do. Harvard Business Review

Imagine you are driving down a dark and lonely road and find yourself caught in white-out snowy conditions. Your headlights are working, but your vision is extremely limited. Your knuckles are white from how hard you are squeezing the steering wheel. You are staring straight ahead, peripheral vision is futile, you are focused just ahead of the headlights fearing something suddenly appears in front of you and you are praying that you can stay on the pavement. You're practically crawling as visibility is measured in inches and feet, not yards or miles.

Does this sound like a fun way to drive? Does your tunnel vision make you more susceptible to things in your periphery that you simply cannot see?

Now, imagine you are in that same car, the weather is clear. The sun is shining, and the sky is as blue as it can be. You have miles of visibility ahead of you.

Do you think you will drive the same way in both circumstances described above? Of course not. In one situation you are cautious, stressed, scared and unable to see more than a millisecond ahead, unable to react in time to hazards that may come your way. In the other situation, with some clarity and certainty, you feel confident on the road ahead. You travel at a reasonable speed to safely reach your destination, and you can see things around you because you don't have to be so laser focused on the unknown, affording you ample time to react if something unexpected arises.

The latter of these two extremes is the journey we seek for you… one with as much certainty as possible without eliminating the flexibility needed to adapt to potential risks and hazards along the way.

The road ahead of you will have many potholes. However, if you have properly considered your plan of travel, understand there are alternative routes you can avail yourself, and you take care to mitigate possible road blocks, you will find the scenery is there for you to enjoy and you will travel at a reasonable speed, delivering you to your ultimate destination on time and in good form.

Certainty provides a backdrop for your decisions that will make your journey as efficient and enjoyable as is possible.

So, jump in and let's go for a ride together and see if we can help clear the view on the other side of *your* windshield.

CHAPTER ONE
A MOUNTAINOUS JOURNEY

Did you know that more people die "descending" Mt. Everest than do from the actual ascent to the Summit?

Imagine you have worked so hard to complete all the pre-climb hurdles, months, if not years, of preparation... you've followed all the rules that you have been taught for survival, and you trudged and toiled successfully, ultimately reaching the Summit…only to meet your maker before returning to base camp below.

Such is life. Sadly, not everyone gets to bask in their glory. What we do know, though, is those who are the best prepared will suffer the least consequence when things get difficult. And while we can't always say when or how, we can almost assure you, things *will* get difficult at some point in your journey ahead.

Your financial life is comprised of three different phases: *the accumulation phase, the distribution phase and the legacy phase.* In our analogy, on this journey to conquer Mt. Everest, we will consider the accumulation phase as the *ascent* up the mountain, the arrival at the doorstep of retirement as *reaching the Summit*, the distribution phase of your financial life will be the *descent* down the mountain and your final pass-through at base camp will be considered your legacy.

When looking at why so many folks have perished on the descent from the mountain, the vast majority either did not bring sufficient supplies, or they were met with unexpected hazards for which they were not sufficiently prepared. The journey down the mountain is not the same as the journey up…the trails are different, as is the weather, and you must be able to think differently to safely navigate your way home.

So too, there are similar issues in our financial lives in terms of preparing for and ultimately enjoying retirement. Some folks don't bring enough supplies (insufficient assets to provide adequate income for an extended period) or they are met with hazards and roadblocks (negative sequence of returns, long term chronic illness, market volatility, tax law changes, health care costs, etc.) for which they did not adequately prepare, resulting in financial consequences that cause overbearing financial difficulties.

Retirement, remember, is a *distribution* phase. To make things work with any sense of certainty requires a different focus. Yes, achieving strong returns on your money can help you meet your needs, but there needs to be consideration for principal and income protection while simultaneously keeping pace with inflation, providing room for changes along the way and very importantly, never running out of money or income - at the very least, not until you run out too.

Remember, *certainty is value* as it ironically delivers flexibility and adaptability, two things that will put icing on your cake when piecing together the puzzle for a healthy retirement plan.

Dave and Rick have been sherpas on this mountain many times and they haven't lost a climber yet. We sincerely hope you enjoy the journey on *your* road ahead.

Sherpa Dave scouting the landscape before Winter arrives

Every journey starts with planning and that includes knowing what you already have to bring along with you and learning what you need to add to *your* backpack to safely *enjoy* the journey or at the least, *survive* the journey. Once you are on the mountain, you're not going to be able to retreat to gather things you hadn't considered before you started. Thorough contemplation of and thoughtful preparation for the eventualities that may come will be key to providing sustainability and efficiency ahead. So, let's get started...

What's in your rucksack?

Mt Everest	Retirement
Rain and Snow Technical Clothing Gear	Social Security Benefits
Undergarments	Employer Pension Benefits
Socks	401(k) assets
Additional layers	IRA assets
Laces	ROTH assets
Polarized sunglasses	SEP assets
Ice climbing cleats	SERP assets/income
Climbing tools and implements	HSA
Oxygen	Medicare Supplements
Food	Expected Inheritance
Water	Non-retirement plan investments
Electrolytes	Liquid assets
Medicine	Guaranteed Lifetime Income plans
First aid kit	Special Needs plans
Tent	Inflation hedge
Sleeping Bag	Wills, Trusts, Power of Attorney
Camera	Health Care Proxy

Map(s)	Long-Term Care expense mitigation
Personal protection	Life Insurance
	Emergency funds

David Kutcher, Sherpa Extraordinaire

CHAPTER TWO

ROADBLOCKS AND TRAIL HAZARDS

"If you can find a path with no obstacles, it probably doesn't lead anywhere."-Frank A. Clark

There will be so many variables and unexpected things that can get in the way as you travel this new road. The impact of some of these hazards far outweigh the good that can come from achieving top returns on your money. It is important to understand this notion since neglecting preparedness for *some* hazards/risks can derail everything you planned, and it won't matter what rate of return you achieve. If you run out of money, the ultimate rate of return is always ZERO, or worse.

While the following list is not exhaustive, it is substantive enough to make the point that there are many, many things that can and will impact your planning. Again, as stated previously, flexibility and adaptability are key and come from adding elements of certainty to your plans.

Here is a partial list of some roadblocks and trail hazards

◊ Negative Sequence of Return

◊ Inflation

◊ Long Term custodial care

◊ Interest rate risk

◊ Investment risk/volatility in general

◊ Longevity Risk

◊ Income and Estate Taxes

◊ Large, unexpected home expenses

- ◊ Estate disposition laws and regulations
- ◊ Unexpected family care-special needs, financial hardship of those you love

While you may not be able to plan for every eventuality that could come your way, some are more manageable than others, but some can be insurmountable without adequate planning.

Next, we take a closer look at the most substantive of these risks and illustrate how understanding them and planning for them might be the most impactful thing you can do to achieve the success you seek in retirement.

CHAPTER THREE

NEGATIVE SEQUENCE OF RETURN

"You can drown in water that averages six inches deep!"

As you begin to piece together your plans for retirement, it is not uncommon for folks to start that process by walking through some simple equations to get to some very basic answers as were highlighted at the beginning of our Prologue…how much will my nest egg be? How much income will that provide? For how long can I expect to draw that income?

The process goes something like this:

◊ We have ‘x" number of dollars saved for retirement today

◊ We can save ‘y" dollars per year between now and retirement start date

◊ We will assume "z" percent annual compound earnings on our money that we have now plus what we invest between now and our retirement start date

- ◊ That will tell us how much money we will have to start our retirement (the nest egg)
- ◊ Next, we will assume a rate of return on our money for the period of time that we will be drawing an income (this will likely be a lower assumed rate as you shift to a more conservative investment approach)
- ◊ And then we will try and determine how much we can withdraw each year from our total savings to enjoy our retirement
- ◊ We will add our other retirement income sources into our planning numbers for things such as social security, municipal and federal government pensions, military and veteran benefits, etc.

That seems simple enough, yes? In theory, that does seem simple enough and a good start to understanding the process ahead. Unfortunately, we need to add several other components to this analysis to provide a reasonable probability of success. Income tax assumptions, inflation assumptions, longevity assumptions just to name a few. And we need to be sure the method used to arrive at an assumed gross rate of return on retirement funds is based on the types of investments that will be used. The point here is that the assumptions plugged into the equations above are the "devil in the details".

One of the biggest mistakes made in backfilling calculations such as we noted above is the use of constant rates of return. What if I earn an average of 5% per year? Or 6% per year? Whatever is determined to be the most prudent rate of return as an assumption, that gets applied as a constant rate in each year of the projections.

Using a constant average rate of return in retirement plan projections ignores the reality of *actual* returns and the *sequence* in which those actual returns might occur. The timing/sequence of the returns is critical to understanding what real-life outcomes may occur and will greatly impact your ability to meet probability expectations in terms of sustaining income for as long as you are alive.

There is a big difference between comparing on paper an average return of 5%, as an example, as compared to *real* returns over a period of time where the ups and downs of the market a*veraged 5%*. When you add the fact that you will be drawing money from your funds to meet your income needs during retirement, the problem of a negative *sequence* of returns becomes as clear as day.

Before we more deeply explore the impact of a negative *sequence* of returns, however, it is important in this exercise that we hammer home the danger in retirement planning when using *average* returns vs. *actual* returns. Remember, average returns on paper do NOT equal real life returns on your money.

EXHIBIT 4.

Average vs. Actual Rates of Return

Average Return		Actual Return
Year 1	-50%	$100,000 ---------------- -$50,000
Year 2 + 50%		$50,000 ------------------ +$25,000 Ending Value = $75,000
Average ROR = 0%		
		Actual ROR = -25%

As you see on the left-hand side of Exhibit 4, in the first year there is a 50% LOSS on investment. In the second year, there is a 50% GAIN. Over the two-year period, *on paper*, this averages a 0% return. An average return of 0%, theoretically, should mean there was no change in your investment account value.

However, as shown on the right-hand side of Exhibit 4, if we had $100,000 invested and it lost 50%, it is then worth $50,000. If the remaining $50,000 then earns a 50% gain in the following year, the total equals the sum of $50,000 multiplied by the 50% gain, which in this case is $25,000, leaving a total of $75,000 from your original $100,000 investment. The ACTUAL return over this two-year period, while *averaging* 0%, *actually* equals a 25% loss on your money.

So, remember, averages do NOT equal actual returns, and this is why we say, ***"you can drown in water that averages 6 inches deep"***.

So, now let's take a closer look at negative sequence of return risk?

Negative Sequence of Return refers to the order in which returns on a portfolio are received. Negative sequence risk can be devastating when poor returns happen early on in the retirement income distribution period, which can significantly reduce the longevity of your portfolio.

Key Points:

1. **Impact of Negative Sequence of Returns:**

   ◊ **Early Losses**: If you experience negative returns early on while simultaneously withdrawing funds, your portfolio shrinks faster, leaving you with less money to benefit from potential future gains.

◊ **Recovery Difficulty**: Recovering from losses becomes more challenging because you have fewer assets left invested and you don't have the luxury of time to allow for recovery.

2. **Mitigating the Risk:**

◊ **Diversification**: Spread investments across different asset classes (stocks, bonds, real estate) to minimize risks.

◊ **Asset Allocation Adjustments**: Adjust asset allocation based on market conditions and personal circumstances.

◊ **Emergency Fund**: Maintain a sufficiently large emergency fund or a separate cash reserve to cover expenses without needing to sell investments during market downturns.

◊ **Flexible Withdrawals**: Be flexible with withdrawal amounts. Reduce withdrawals during years when the market is down.

◊ **Income-Producing Investments**: Invest in assets that provide steady income (like dividends, interest) to reduce the need to sell investments during downturns.

◊ **Annuities**: Consider annuities to provide guaranteed income, reducing reliance on portfolio withdrawals.

◊ **Professional Advice**: Seek advice from financial sherpas to tailor strategies specific to your needs.

By understanding and preparing for the sequence of returns risk, you can better protect your investment portfolio, *especially* during retirement years.

In the next exhibit, the comparison of two scenarios is eye opening to say the least. We are showing you a period over which the same exact rates of return are achieved, the same exact income is distributed, and the same exact starting value is used. The ONLY difference between Portfolio A and Portfolio B is the *sequence* in which the returns are achieved.

EXHIBIT 5.

Sequence of Returns with Withdrawals

Age	Annual Return	Annual Withdrawal End of Year	Portfolio A Year-end Values Beginning of Year	Age	Annual Return	Annual Withdrawal End of Year	Portfolio B Year-end Values Beginning of Year
65	N/A	$ 25,000	$ 500,000	65	N/A	$ 25,000	$ 500,000
66	-10.10%	$ 25,000	$ 427,025	66	19.40%	$ 25,000	$ 567,150
67	-13.00%	$ 25,000	$ 349,762	67	9.50%	$ 25,000	$ 593,654
68	-23.40%	$ 25,000	$ 248,768	68	-0.70%	$ 25,000	$ 564,674
69	26.40%	$ 25,000	$ 282,842	69	11.40%	$ 25,000	$ 601,196
70	9.00%	$ 25,000	$ 281,048	70	29.60%	$ 25,000	$ 746,751
71	3.00%	$ 25,000	$ 263,729	71	13.40%	$ 25,000	$ 818,465
72	13.60%	$ 25,000	$ 271,197	72	0.00%	$ 25,000	$ 793,465
73	3.50%	$ 25,000	$ 254,813	73	12.80%	$ 25,000	$ 866,829
74	-38.50%	$ 25,000	$ 141,335	74	23.50%	$ 25,000	$ 1,039,659
75	23.50%	$ 25,000	$ 143,674	75	-38.50%	$ 25,000	$ 624,015
76	12.80%	$ 25,000	$ 133,864	76	3.50%	$ 25,000	$ 619,981
77	0.00%	$ 25,000	$ 108,864	77	13.60%	$ 25,000	$ 675,898
78	13.40%	$ 25,000	$ 95,102	78	3.00%	$ 25,000	$ 670,425
79	29.60%	$ 25,000	$ 90,852	79	9.00%	$ 25,000	$ 703,513
80	11.40%	$ 25,000	$ 73,360	80	26.40%	$ 25,000	$ 857,640
81	-0.70%	$ 25,000	$ 48,021	81	-23.40%	$ 25,000	$ 637,803
82	9.50%	$ 25,000	$ 25,208	82	-13.00%	$ 25,000	$ 533,138
83	19.40%	$ 25,000	$ 248	83	-10.10%	$ 25,000	$ 456,816
	Average	Total	Balance		Average	Total	Balance
	4.97%	$ 475,000	$ 248		4.97%	$ 475,000	$ 456,816

Huge Difference

For illustrative purposes only. This does not represent any particular investment
Returns do not include fees and deductions inherent in investing

In Exhibit 5, we are comparing the impact of the *sequence* of the returns.

Everything else is the same between Portfolio A, on the left-hand side of the chart, and Portfolio B, on the right-hand side of the chart.

◊ The starting Value is $500,000 on both sides

◊ The Annual Withdrawal is $25,000 on both sides

◊ The rates of return are the same EXCEPT they come in *reverse order*, both *averaging* 4.97% over the period shown.

As you can see, while all else was the same except for the *sequence* of the returns, there is a huge difference in the ending values. The owner of Portfolio A has run out of money, while the owner of Portfolio B has almost the same amount of money remaining as when they started.

Now that you have seen the impact of a negative sequence of returns and the danger in forecasting retirement income plans using constant average rates of return versus actual or at least historical rates of return, your next natural question is going to be, "what can I do to help avoid this risk?".

Things you can do to help manage sequence of return risk

Having a bucket of money that is not correlated to the stock market, often called a "cash reserve" or "safe bucket", is a strategic way to provide investment safety during retirement, particularly in the context of a negative sequence of return risk. Here's how this approach can help:

Key Benefits:

1. **Protection During Market Downturns:**

    ◊ In the event of a market downturn, if your primary investment portfolio (stocks, bonds) performs poorly, having a separate reserve of stable assets allows you to avoid withdrawing from investments at a loss.

2. **Liquidity and Stability:**

    ◊ A cash reserve provides liquidity and ensures that you have readily accessible funds to cover your living expenses without needing to sell assets from your investment portfolio at depressed prices.

3. **Reduced Market Exposure:**

◊ By having money in assets that are not correlated with the stock market (e.g., cash, money market funds, short-term bonds, fixed annuities, life insurance cash value), you reduce your overall market exposure during volatile periods.

4. **Flexibility in Withdrawal:**

◊ The presence of a non-correlated bucket allows you to exercise flexibility in terms of which assets to withdraw from, enabling you to time the market better and mitigate losses.

5. **Psychological Comfort:**

◊ Knowing that you have a reserve can provide peace of mind and reduce anxiety during market downturns, allowing for a more disciplined investment strategy without panic selling.

Implementing a Non-Correlated Bucket Strategy

1. **Initial Allocation:**

◊ Determine a portion of your retirement portfolio that should be allocated to non-correlated assets. This amount can vary but commonly ranges from 3 to 7 years' worth of living expenses. (In theory, you want a year's worth of income for each year in the future that you might need to cover negative investment results)

2. **Types of Non-Correlated Assets:**

◊ **Cash**: The most liquid form, providing immediate access to funds. (Typically, will receive the lowest rate of return)

- ◊ **Money Market Accounts**: Slightly higher yield than cash while maintaining liquidity.
- ◊ **Short-term Bonds**: Lower volatility compared to longer-term bonds, offering more stability.
- ◊ **Certificates of Deposit (CDs)**: Longer-term CDs can offer a better return than cash or money markets, though with early withdrawal penalties.
- ◊ **Fixed annuities:** Fixed and Fixed Indexed Annuities when designed properly can provide respectable rates of return while protecting your principal from any investment related loss.
- ◊ **Fixed Permanent Life Insurance:** Certain types of permanent life insurance can provide significant value, serving as an alternative pool of funds for use when markets turn downward. You can gain access to cash values within the policy on a tax-free basis if structured properly and the policy performance in terms of *long-term* earnings should mimic CD type rates of return. Not to mention the income tax free death benefit to help preserve or create your financial legacy

3. **Replenishing the Reserve:**
   - ◊ During times of market growth, consider taking a portion of the gains from your portfolio to replenish or increase your non-correlated bucket.
4. **Review Periodically:**
   - ◊ Periodically review and adjust the size of your cash reserve based on changes in your living expenses, interest rates, inflation, and overall market conditions.

By integrating a non-correlated bucket into your retirement strategy, you build a buffer against negative sequence of return risk, ensuring that your retirement years are financially secure and less vulnerable to the unpredictable nature of market fluctuations. Note, you're beginning to provide some certainty in an uncertain world.

In Exhibit 6 we are illustrating how the use of a non-correlated bucket of money for use during market downturns can significantly improve your outlook for sustaining enough funds to carry you through your lifetime.

EXHIBIT 6.

		Josh and Mary			Bill and Margo	
Year	S&P 500	Annual Withdrawal	Account Balance	S&P 500	Annual Withdrawal	Account Balance
		$ 50,000	$ 1,000,000		$ 50,000	$ 800,000
2000	-9.11%	$ 50,000	$ 863,455	-9.11%	$ 50,000	$ 681,675
2001	-11.89%	$ 50,000	$ 716,735	-11.89%	$ -	$ 600,624
2002	-22.10%	$ 50,000	$ 519,387	-22.10%	$ -	$ 467,886
2003	28.68%	$ 50,000	$ 604,007	28.68%	$ -	$ 602,076
2004	10.88%	$ 50,000	$ 614,283	10.88%	$ 50,000	$ 612,142
2005	4.91%	$ 50,000	$ 591,989	4.91%	$ 50,000	$ 589,743
2006	15.79%	$ 50,000	$ 627,569	15.79%	$ 50,000	$ 624,968
2007	5.49%	$ 50,000	$ 609,278	5.49%	$ 50,000	$ 606,534
2008	-37.00%	$ 50,000	$ 352,345	-37.00%	$ 50,000	$ 350,616
2009	26.46%	$ 50,000	$ 382,345	26.46%	$ -	$ 443,389
2010	15.06%	$ 50,000	$ 382,397	15.06%	$ 50,000	$ 452,634
2011	2.11%	$ 50,000	$ 339,410	2.11%	$ 50,000	$ 411,129
2012	16.00%	$ 50,000	$ 335,716	16.00%	$ 50,000	$ 418,910
2013	32.39%	$ 50,000	$ 378,259	32.39%	$ 50,000	$ 488,400
2014	13.69%	$ 50,000	$ 373,198	13.69%	$ 50,000	$ 498,417
2015	1.38%	$ 50,000	$ 327,658	1.38%	$ 50,000	$ 454,605
2016	11.96%	$ 50,000	$ 310,866	11.96%	$ 50,000	$ 452,996
2017	21.83%	$ 50,000	$ 317,813	21.83%	$ 50,000	$ 490,970
2018	-4.38%	$ 50,000	$ 256,083	-4.38%	$ 50,000	$ 421,655
2019	31.49%	$ 50,000	$ 270,978	31.49%	$ 50,000	$ 488,690
Totals:		$ 1,000,000	$ 270,978		$ 800,000	$ 488,690
Average:	7.68%			7.68%		

With Bill and Margo avoiding withdrawals from the investment account in each year following poor investment results they have $217,712 more money at the end of the 20 year period shown.

Bill and Margo used their non-correlated bucket to provide income during those other years Total income over the twent year period is the same for both couples.

Exhibit 6 continued...

Josh and Mary, who are represented on the left-hand side of this chart, arrived at the summit with $1,000,000 in funds invested in a managed portfolio dedicated to their retirement income. Their annual income needs are $50,000 per year to be added to their two social security incomes. Unfortunately, Josh and Mary have little money outside of the retirement plan funds identified above, and so this money was the sole source of income besides social security, to meet their income objectives.

{Knowledge check point: It is important for you to make a mental note at this point that while the twenty-year average return shown in Exhibit 6 is 7.68% and the rate of annual distribution for income is 5% ($50,000 on a $1,000,000 portfolio), the portfolio is losing money. It should, in theory, be growing by the 2.68% difference between the rate of return and the rate of distribution...the reason it is not growing is exactly what we described in the discussion on averages and negative sequence of return.}

Even with decent overall returns, selling off investments at inopportune times leaves them with a declining balance that may not last as long as they do. Also note that this projection assumes a constant income of $50,000 which does nothing to account for inflation. In real life it is unlikely either of the couples used in this example would be satisfied with this static income amount. Increasing distributions to account for inflation exacerbates the issue we are illustrating here. Real-life planning should accommodate and plan for inflation adjusted income needs.

In contrast to Josh and Mary, Bill and Margo, represented on the right-hand side of this chart, created a non-correlated side fund with approximately $200,000 prior to retirement. Their total funds available at retirement are the same as Josh and Mary, but they chose to create a combination of the non-correlated bucket alongside the managed investment portfolio. They've given themselves choices as to which resources they will use to meet their annual income objectives. Otherwise, these two couples have similar situations.

As you can see, because Bill and Margo are able to avoid having to take income from the investment account at inopportune times, they increased their projected outcome over and above Josh and Mary by $217,712. ($488,690-$270,978 =$217,712) and they did so with a starting value in the investment portfolio of $200,000 less than Josh and Mary. This increase in available funds for Bill and Margo in future years was done WITHOUT sacrificing any annual income along the way…they received $200,000 less from the investment portfolio than Josh and Mary, but they made up for that with $200,000 from their non-correlated bucket of money.

The additional funds in Bill and Margo's investment account are what may very well be their insurance that they will not outlive their income. (Certainty)

As shown previously in this chapter, the type of financial instrument that Bill and Margo choose to use for their non-correlated bucket could have been one of many choices or even a combination of solutions. There are many factors that would come into play as to which type might best serve your needs…this is something you can hammer out with your financial sherpa.

What did we learn or confirm here?

1. Using average returns can be misleading at best
2. Negative sequence of returns is a very real risk to meeting probability expectations in terms of maintaining sufficient assets to produce sufficient income for your entire lifetime(s)
3. There are several ways to mitigate the sequence of return risk and the earlier you seek to incorporate this type of component in your plans, the more choices you will have as to what might bring the most value to your overall goals and objectives

CHAPTER FOUR

INFLATION

Inflation is a prevalent topic in general. People know what it is for the most part and understand it isn't a good thing when it comes to purchasing power. Yet, the impact that inflation can have when considering long-term retirement projections is often underestimated. Applying a blanket assumption of an inflation rate across all financial considerations can be as dangerous as using level, constant average rates of return in your investment return projections, as we discussed in the prior chapter.

We must be careful when planning for inflation that we use assumptions that closely match the specific things we are concerned with. Basing everything in your planning on the published Consumer Price Index (CPI) can lead to inadequate or faulty planning. The CPI does NOT necessarily represent *you* and your consumer needs and wants. Your consumption may be more highly impacted by inflationary factors than someone else and your planning for possible road hazards ahead should consider how inflation is impacting the very hazards you are considering.

As an example, the cost of long-term custodial care has risen significantly faster in the U.S. than the general Consumer Price

Index (CPI). This means the price of long-term care services such as nursing home care increases at a much higher rate compared to the overall cost of goods and services in the economy. Demand is increasing and the labor costs associated in the healthcare sector of the economy push the rising costs of care beyond that of the more general CPI. When planning financially for potential long-term care needs, this is an important item to keep in mind.

Key points about long-term care costs vs. CPI:

◊ **Higher inflation rate:**

Studies consistently show that the inflation rate for long-term care is considerably higher than the general CPI, often exceeding the inflation rate for medical care as well.

◊ **Demographics:**

An aging population is a key component resulting in increased demand for long-term care, contributing to price increases.

◊ **Labor costs:**

Service pricing reflects the growing demand for specialized care which is leading to higher labor costs.

In your specific planning, it is important to understand *your* own needs and wants and what the consumer costs will be for someone who lives their life as you do.

In general, however, what we are looking at in terms of inflation is to be sure we are accounting for rises in the cost of goods and services that *you will use* in your daily life and understanding that any rise in those costs reduces the value of the dollar you are spending to get those goods and services. If your financial assumptions don't account for this, you will eventually find that you can't meet your needs and wants any longer without taking on additional risk.

To help understand the impact inflation can have on your money over time, let's use a simple rule in math called the rule of 72.

What is the Rule of 72?

In finance, the Rule of 72 is a formula that estimates the amount of time it takes for an investment to double in value, earning a fixed annual rate of return and assuming compounding earnings. The simple calculation involves dividing 72 by the annual interest rate. It, conversely, can tell us how long before something is worth ½ of what it is worth today.

As an example, if we are assuming a 6% rate of return, we divide 72 by 6 and the result is 12. So, $1 will grow to $2 at a 6% rate of return over a 12-year period. Or, if you have $100,000 in a particular investment and you are assuming it will earn 6% per year compounded, it will be worth $200,000 in 12 years. Simple enough, yes?

Conversely, $1 will be worth $ .50 in 12 years, assuming a 6% rate of inflation. In other words, the buying power of your dollar today will be cut in half 12 years from now assuming the costs of goods and services has risen at 6% per year.

With the rule of 72 at your fingertips, you can easily estimate the inflationary assumptions of specific eventualities such as the cost of long-term custodial care mentioned above. Let's do some quick math here on the assumption of long-term care costs based upon those specific expenses versus the general CPI.

The Consumer Price Index (CPI) for All Urban Consumers (CPI-U) in February 2025 was 319.09, which is a 3.0% increase from one year ago. (Bureau of Labor Statistics) With longer term inflation reported just under 3%, we will leave our example at 3% for easy numbers.

Estimates for rising costs associated with Long Term Care expenses, depending upon exactly which services you are measuring, hover around 5-6%. We will use the 6% rate, again, just for illustrative purposes.

So, if you assume the average annual cost of long-term care today is $100,000 and you are 60 years old, then at age 72, 12 years from now, assuming a rise in costs of 6% per year, your average annual cost of care will be $200,000. And at age 84, twelve years later and at a time when you are more likely to be seeking this type of care, the costs would be projected to be $400,000 per year.

If we then apply the average stay or length of time someone needs care, which is approximately 2.5 years, we are facing a potential financial event that could cost upward of $1,000,000 per spouse. $400,000 per year X 2.5 years = $1,000,000.

Making the same projection based upon the general CPI of 3% would have had you planning to mitigate an event projected to be ½ of what it truly might be…and planning for a financial event that could cost each spouse $500,000, only to find out it actually is going to cost $1,000,000 is no small mistake. These are the types of things that can make or break the best laid plans.

You should be applying inflationary pressure in all of your assumptions, meaning you need to trim expected returns to compensate for increases in the cost of living the same way you have to compensate for taxes on your various retirement income sources. A 6% rate of return in a 20% tax bracket yields a spendable income equivalent to a 4.8% rate of return, net of taxes. Similarly, a 6% rate of return is diminished by the cost of living since the buying power of your dollar is going down as inflation rises.

As you consider the returns required to help meet your goals and objectives or when you are forecasting projected asset growth, it is vital to include inflation in your plans.

To help keep pace with inflation it is essential that at least some component of your money earns a higher rate of return than the inflation rate, and overall, you want your combined return on all investments to outperform the impact inflation is projected to have on your buying power in the years ahead. In general, this means you can't rely solely on cash-equivalent investments, when adjusted for taxes they will not keep pace with inflation. There are ways to help mitigate this issue without taking on substantial risk. We will be looking at this conceptually in the chapters ahead. In general, it is likely you will need exposure to a diversified investment portfolio which will bear some risk but offer you the best long term rates of return and you will couple that with options for the non-correlated assets we discussed previously...since your overall return needs to try and outpace inflation, the more net return you can garner from your non-correlated bucket means the less risk you will need to take in the investment portfolio to keep pace overall. Remember, the decent from the mountain (distribution phase) tends to be better served with less volatility. Keeping risk levels appropriate for this time in your life is more easily achieved when the non-correlated assets are providing decent rates

What did we learn or confirm here?

1. Inflation can have a significant impact on buying power over time
2. Expected returns on assets need to be adjusted to account for inflation
3. The CPI does not represent many things being considered in broad-based retirement planning
4. Long Term Care costs are rising at approximately twice the rate of the CPI

INTERLUDE

THE LONG WAY HOME

Living longer sounds like a great thing on the surface, and to be honest it is hard to find fault in that thinking. Longer life expectancy promises more time with our loved ones, being here for more grandchildren and having time to enjoy them, more time to travel, more leisure time and the list goes on. What's not to like about that?

But in life, and specifically with longevity, rewards tend to come with additional risk.

The long trail home brings with it more imminent health issues, requiring professional care and maintenance which translates to higher out of pocket medical costs. Our money needs to last longer while at the same time we are likely needing to increase our distribution rate and all of this while the dreaded storm of needing long term custodial care looms large on the horizon.

Some of you have seen this happening with your own parents. Mom and/or Dad become more sedentary, physical and/or mental capabilities suffer and soon enough the aged can no longer perform, without assistance, some of the six basic activities of daily living: eating, bathing, dressing, grooming, transferring, toileting. Their medical bills have eroded their funds unexpectedly and perhaps you have had to find ways to help them meet their daily living expenses.

So, yes, the idea of living longer brings with it many positive opportunities, but it also brings with it the risk of the single most concerning road hazard you will likely encounter on your descent. It happens often and it can be fatal to your financial well-being.

Here are some statistics just for reference and you can find more detailed information at the links noted below.

According to the Social Security Administration Period Life Table, 2022

◊ A 65-year-old male has a life expectancy of 17.48 years (Age 82.48) and a probability of death within 1 year of .017897

◊ A 65-year-old female has a life expectancy of 20.12 years (Age 85.12) and a probability of death within 1 year of .011018

◊ A 70-year-old male 14.09 (Age 84.09)

◊ A 70-year-old female 16.27 (Age 86.27)

Just as you will see in chapters ahead that geographic location will likely influence various components of retirement planning, State specific life expectancy differs from the broader Social Security based stats above.

As an example, in Rhode Island, ranked 8th in the country for life expectancy, a 65-year-old male has a life expectancy to age 75.9 and a 65-year-old female to age 81. In Alaska, ranked 39th in the country for life expectancy, a 65-year-old male has a life expectancy to age 72.2 and a 65-year-old female to age 77.3.

Rick likes to kiddingly say that while folks in Alaska seem to have the platform to live longer by living off grid, unplugged and less stressful along with plentiful access to some of the healthiest food you can eat, that obviously doesn't outweigh the increased probability of you being eaten by a bear or run over by a moose. In all seriousness, though, your environment does impact life expectancy.

In your personal planning, you should additionally consider your family history as well as your current health, and while genetics can play a big role in longevity expectations, take care to consider how or why a parent may have had a premature death as there were many environmental factors that don't exist for you today that may have played a big part in their cause of death.

Beyond facing the risk of having to bear the cost of long-term custodial care when considering your potential life expectancy, maintaining the longevity of your retirement funds in order for them to continue to provide you income can also be a daunting task. In many, many cases, income planning includes the distribution of both earnings as well as your principal sum of assets to meet your annual income needs. Trying to guess how long the nest egg needs to last is risky business and being wrong can have catastrophic results.

In understanding the power of insurance based financial solutions, where mortality risk is shared across thousands of people, you can produce predictable solutions and transfer the risk elsewhere of running out of income producing assets. We often find the use of guaranteed lifetime income programs to be of significant value as just one component of a broader overall solution.

Here are some sources for your review if you wish to see more detailed life expectancy statistics.

Social Security Administration Period Life Table, 2022

https://www.ssa.gov/oact/STATS/table4c6.html

Table A. National Vital Statistics Reports Volume 74, Number 7 April 8, 2025

https://www.cdc.gov/nchs/data/nvsr/nvsr74/nvsr74-02.pdf

Table A. National Vital Statistics Reports Volume 73, Number 7 August 21, 2024 https://www.cdc.gov/nchs/data/nvsr/nvsr73/nvsr73-07.pdf

What did we learn or confirm here?

1. Living longer than our parents is a very real and almost certain probability
2. Living longer has many, many rewards but also subjects us to many more financial risks
3. The longer you live, the more susceptible you are to higher health care costs for regular maintenance
4. The longer you live, the higher the probability that you will require long-term custodial care
5. The longer you live, the higher the risk that you will run out of money
6. There are ways to mitigate the financial risks associated with increased longevity

Longevity...

Jo's Golden Delight(background) and Bobbie Socks(foreground), Foster, RI

The buckskin quarter horse mare pictured above in the background at Rick's farm, formally registered as Jos Golden Delight, but more affectionately known as Josie, is seen here a couple of years before she passed away. While it was wonderful to have Josie live for so many years, 36 to be exact, her last few years posed challenges with her health that had not been seen before. Josie was one of those horses that had a very strong constitution. She was never sick! While she *was* well taken care of, eventually age took its toll. She began to lose her teeth and ultimately the ability to chew her food. In time, she just couldn't get the nutrition she needed to keep on keeping on.

Over the last 12 or so months of Josie's life, her need for more precise care, supplemental nutrition and more frequent visits from the vet were needed. It was wonderful to have her with us for so long, but the reality of aging, and in her case far outliving life expectancy, meant significantly higher costs to keep her comfortable.

The joys and rewards of living long come with increased probability of needing special care and special care typically comes with increased costs. This is true whether we are talking about our pets or our family members.

CHAPTER FIVE

LONG TERM CARE

The risk of having to fund for an extended long-term care event for either spouse or both is the single highest financial risk you will face in the next 20-30 years. Let's look at some statistics and see if we can put a dollar amount on this potential hazard.

The statistical risks associated with the need for long-term care are based on various factors including age, gender, family history, and lifestyle. Here's a concise overview:

◊ **Age**: The risk of needing long-term care increases with age. Around 70% of people over the age of 65 will require *some* type of long-term care services during their lifetime.

◊ **Gender**: Women are typically at a higher risk than men due to their longer life expectancy. Statistically, over 70% of nursing home residents are women.

◊ **Family History**: A family history of chronic conditions or disabilities can increase the likelihood of needing long-term care.

- ◊ **Lifestyle and Health Factors**: Obesity, smoking, and lack of exercise can increase the risk of chronic illnesses that may require long-term care.
- ◊ **Living Situation**: People living alone may need professional long-term care, as they might lack informal support from family.

These factors contribute to the probability of needing long-term care, highlighting the importance of planning and considering insurance or other financial strategies to manage potential future needs.

The **average cost of long-term care in the U.S.** can vary widely depending on the type and location of care. Here are some general estimates:

- ◊ **Nursing Home Care**: The average cost is around $100,000 per year for a private room and about $90,000 for a shared room.
- ◊ **Assisted Living Facility**: The average cost is approximately $4,500 per month, totaling around $54,000 annually.
- ◊ **Home Care Services**: The cost for a home health aide average is around $25 per hour, which can quickly add up depending on the level of care required.
- ◊ **Adult Day Care Services**: These services are more budget-friendly, averaging about $75 per day.

These costs can vary significantly based upon geographical location, the level of care required, and other factors. It's crucial to plan accordingly.

The **average cost of long-term care in Alaska** is generally higher than the national average due to its remote location and higher cost of living. Here are some estimates:

1. **Nursing Home Care:** The average cost is approximately $375,000 per year for a private room and slightly less for a shared room.

2. **Assisted Living Facility:** The cost is about $6,830 per month, which totals around $81,960 annually.

3. **Home Care Services:** A home health aide costs approximately $30 per hour.

These figures can vary based on specific locations within Alaska and the individual care needs. The higher costs underscore the importance of financial planning for long-term care in the region.

To offer some contrast and confirm the variances in costs geographically, here are some numbers from Rick's backyard. In **Rhode Island, the average costs of long-term care** are as follows:

1. **Nursing Home Care:** The average cost is approximately $120,000 to $140,000 per year for a private room.

2. **Assisted Living Facility:** The cost averages around $4,900 per month, totaling about $58,800 annually.

3. **Home Care Services:** The cost for a home health aide is about $28 per hour.

The statistical information provided above is easily gathered from an internet search. Numbers may vary a bit from source to source, but they are close enough that we can use these numbers to do some prognosticating for the "what if?"

The probability of needing care that will incur expenses is at about 50%. Meaning 1 in every 2 people over age 65 will need some form of long-term care that requires professional assistance and/or facility-based living.

The average long-term care event lasts approximately 2.5 years. Physical issues will result in shorter periods of care and cognitive issues tend to result in much longer periods of care, in some cases 5-7 years or more.

The Average cost of a nursing home in the US hovers around $125,000 annually.

Average cost today: $125,000

Average period of time needed: 2.5 years

$125,000 X 2.5 = $312,500 exposure in year 2025 dollars

It would be atypical for someone to experience long-term care expense events early on in their retirement, although these things do occur occasionally. But most events are going to be in someone's late seventies and older. In our example, let's assume an event at age 80 and assume we are 65 years old today. That means we need to think ahead and plan for the inflation adjusted cost of the financial exposure we see today.

If we use $312,500 from our calculation above and adjust it over 15 years at 6% inflation, that exposure is $706,532 per spouse. If we are considering this risk for a married couple, this is now $706,532 X 2 = $1,413,065 in total.

That is almost $1,500,000 in financial exposure for a retiring couple, and it doesn't account for locations with higher costs, such as Alaska, and it doesn't account for the potentially longer-term risk associated with cognitive decline such as dementia and Alzheimer's.

The financial impact of an unplanned event such as we are talking about here can be devastating. This may, in fact, be an unpassable roadblock. When a storm like this hits, even if you are somewhat prepared, it will challenge your resources and potentially outlast your ability to stay hunkered down.

To lessen the impact of potential long-term care expenses, there are many choices up for consideration today. Far more than were available just ten years ago. It is important to understand, however, that each of these choices has their own respective set of rules and guidelines and you may or may not qualify for everything you may wish to consider. As an example, most solutions have age limits to access new coverage. You can't wait until you need it as you will either be too old to get it or not healthy enough to qualify.

This is a financial risk you want to get out ahead of...you will want the benefit of as many choices as possible so that you can build or design a plan that best fits your own objectives.

Long-Term Care Insurance: Purchasing a long-term care insurance policy can help cover the costs associated with assisted living, nursing home care, and home health care. It's best to buy a policy when you're younger and in good health to secure lower premiums.

> Individual Long-Term Care (LTC) Insurance was the go-to financial protection vehicle for several years. But pricing issues and rising costs have narrowed the offerings available today specific to *individual* LTC plans and the plans are less desirable than they were previously. It would be rare today

for us to consider these plans in our work with our clients. There are far too many other options, in our opinion, that provide a better overall solution to help mitigate this risk

1. **Health Savings Accounts (HSAs):** Contributing to an HSA allows you to use pre-tax dollars for qualifying medical expenses, including some long-term care costs. Funds roll over year-to-year and can grow tax-free. This can be an effective method if saving to these accounts starts early enough and at a high enough level to provide substantive funds if needed. However, this is a dollar-for-dollar option that we consider to be in the "self-funding" category, which may not provide enough benefits when needed.

2. **Medicaid Planning:** Medicaid can cover long-term care costs for those who qualify. Planning ahead can help you meet eligibility requirements through asset protection strategies. While we note this as a possible solution, it is rare in our market that we are planning to deplete assets to a point of qualifying for Medicaid. We would like to note here that variances in Medicaid benefits do exist across different states. From our observation, Alaska has a fairly liberal Medicaid offering, particularly in terms of how they treat the spouse of a Medicaid applicant.

3. **Veterans Benefits:** If you are a veteran, you may qualify for long-term care benefits through the Department of Veterans Affairs, which can help reduce out-of-pocket costs.

4. **Investment and Savings Strategy:** Regularly setting aside funds in a diversified investment portfolio or a dedicated savings account for future long-term care expenses can provide a financial cushion. This concept is like using an HSA account noted above. You are funding your own pool of money,

self-insuring, so to speak. Again, you are planning to pay dollar for dollar in these situations.

5. **Family Assistance:** Discussing care plans with family members may result in shared responsibilities, reducing the need for paid services. If you have the right type of coverage, you can even arrange to pay a family member to help…this can be very helpful in situations where someone willing and able to help cannot do so if having to give up their own income to help.
6. **HYDRID Life Insurance with Long-Term Care Riders:** Some life insurance policies offer riders that cover long-term care expenses, providing additional resources when needed. Others build chronic illness benefits into their base plans.

Unbeknownst to many people, many of today's life insurance plans can provide "living" benefits too. These plans are no longer just for those you leave behind. In essence, the plans allow for use of the death benefit while you are alive and needing long term care services.

HYBRID life insurance plans that provide living benefits for chronic, critical and terminal care come in many different flavors today. Some are funded with single premiums, others with short premium paying periods and others that allow for premiums to be spread out over your lifetime. Some provide benefits via a *reimbursement method* and therefore reimburse expenses as they are submitted for actual care and others provide benefits via an *indemnity method* which more simply provides a cash benefit each month if you qualify for care by meeting the definition of being chronically ill.

Virtually all these plans use the same definition to determine if you are eligible for benefits; the inability to perform two or more activities of daily living for 90 days or more-whether that be from physical or cognitive decline.

7. **Long Term Care Annuities**

    Similarly to the HYBRID life insurance plans, there are annuities today that have a hybrid design to provide mitigation for long term care expenses.

The primary value in either of the last two options noted, HYBRID Life and LTC Annuities, is that each of them provides benefits on a *leveraged* basis, meaning any money paid into these plans is leveraged to provide benefits that are more meaningful than the dollar- for-dollar, self-funding, options mentioned previously. So, $1 into a plan may provide $3-$4 out in the form of LTC benefits. And, if the benefits for LTC are never needed, only partially needed or if entire circumstances change, the dollars that are allocated to these hybrid plans have not gone for naught, as it would have done under the old individual LTC policies. Some, if not all, of the funding will be available separately as a benefit to the family or the retiree, one way or another.

This last point is the biggest difference between more contemporary solutions and the traditional individual LTC insurance policies you may or may not be familiar with. In the traditional individual LTC policies, if you never need the benefits or only partially need the benefits, you can't recover your funding or make other use of it. Premiums paid will have been a pure expense on your retirement funds and for no reason. While some individual plans will include what they call non-forfeiture benefits, this is not quite the same as having options for premium refunds and other important "plan B" offerings…again, we like to know there is flexibility and room to re-purpose if things change in the future. (Control)

Considering your options along with a financial sherpa can help you create a comprehensive plan to manage potential long-term care costs effectively.

In many situations, plan design incorporates the use of the on-going income projections of a retirement plan and seeks to fill *the gap* between a portion, or all the household income, and the projected cost of care.

Rick likes to use the situation from when his Dad was alive to illustrate this point.

Dad very much wanted to leave as much net estate to Rick and his two sisters as he possibly could. Not that any of that was necessary, but it was important to Dad and so the plan was to cover any potential LTC monthly expense by using a *combination* of his continuing income such as social security/pension benefits along with LTC benefits that will be provided by an individual LTC policy, while also preserving any principal balance he had in his accounts such as his IRA. Other income such as Required Minimum distributions from an IRA will provide some buffer and pay some household expenses that will continue-whether he is receiving care at home or in a facility.

Dad's recurring income was approximately $5,000 per month, Mom had already passed on, so the income to the household was solely for Dad. In other words, we did not need to worry about income continuing to the household for anyone else such as a healthy spouse if Dad was receiving care. His major expenses were out of the way with no mortgage and no other debt.

Dad purchased an individual LTC policy with a monthly benefit of $6,000.

The year Dad passed away, the cost of a private room in a nursing home here in RI was approximately $11,000 per month. As you can see, between the pension income and the LTC policy benefits, essentially, the entire cost of Long-Term Care for Dad would be covered each month and allow for any of his remaining assets to pass to us children at his death. The plan seemed good to go.

As it turned out, Dad's stay in a nursing home was very limited and he passed away inside of Medicare's 100-day coverage limitation. So, there was never a need to pay the nursing home -however, had he lasted just a few more weeks he would have been relying on his pension and LTC policy to cover the bill, and it would have done so perfectly. There was no need to buy a policy covering $11,000 per month when we had enough other income to meet the costs, had they occurred.

Let's take a closer look at some other alternatives available today.

The following exhibit shows three alternatives for Joseph. The following exhibit shows three alternatives for Joseph, a 74-year-old male in relatively good health. His wife, Cindy, has some current health issues that preclude her from securing LTC coverage at this time, but the husband wants to try and leave some legacy to his children and so he wants to try and do his best to mitigate any potential threat if he needs care.

He has approximately $100,000 in discretionary assets to allocate to this endeavor and we want to try and get as much LTC coverage out of that funding as we can, but not at the complete or exorbitant sacrifice of benefits if an event never occurs. If things change otherwise, he wants some flexibility and he would want as much to pass to his heirs as is possible. Joseph and Cindy live a modest lifestyle, they do not have any government or private pensions other than social security and they sustain their financial life from the required minimum distributions on Joseph's IRA. Joseph and Cindy live in Alaksa and are aware of the costs in Alaska in comparison to elsewhere in the lower 48 states. Joseph is also well aware that if he were to need formal care for any extended period of time, he does not have the resources to cover those expenses…this is a situation where he is simply trying to protect whatever he can if care *is* needed and ultimately preserve as much of his estate for his two children as he can. There are not enough resources to cover a full-blown long-term care event.

Again, Joseph has made available approximately $100,000 in liquid funds to try and cover as much of this potential risk as he can without completely giving up control of the funds or losing everything if care is not needed. At the time this book is being written, interest rates are still higher than they have been for years and there are some guaranteed programs where we can increase the value of the $100,000 in terms of its buying power. In other words, instead of trading the entire $100,000 of funding for a Long Term Care Plan, we are looking at programs that will turn the $100,000 into a stream of income for the next ten years, together with a guaranteed interest rate (5 %-6%)and if Joseph were to die before funding is completed, his estate will benefit from any remaining funds that were being otherwise allocated to the original funding plan for the LTC plan.

By doing so, we can guarantee that the $100,000 will generate an annual income of $12,334 for the next ten years. (See the two plans on the right-hand side of Exhibit 7) We have turned the

$100,000 in funding into $123, 340. We are getting more using this strategy than if we simply deposited the $100,000 as single pay funding to an LTC plan.

Joseph was less concerned with being able to maintain access to his full $100,000 funding and was more concerned with either generating a potential Long Term Care Benefit or leaving as much as he can to his children. In this situation, we are using a hybrid life insurance plan that includes Long Term Care benefits.

The Death Benefit and the Long-Term Care benefits are generally paid income tax free. Since Joseph's estate consists primarily of the residence and his IRA account, his beneficiaries, at his death, will have income taxes to pay on any remaining funds in his IRA. The Income Tax free death benefit can go a long way to compensate for that income tax, allowing him to leave a larger net estate to his two children than he would be able to do otherwise.

Getting back to the funding mechanism in this situation, any dollar remaining unused during the first ten years reverts back to his beneficiaries should Joseph die between now and age 84. This potential unused funding is NOT reflected in the death benefit numbers shown in Exhibit 7.

Exhibit 7.

Long Term Care Analysis

Client Names:	Male Non Smoker Age 74			
	Ten Pay Solutions			
PRODUCT:	XYZ Company	ABC Company	123 Company -Standard Rates	123 Company-Preferred rates
Annual Ten Pay Premium	$ 12,000	$ 12,000	$ 12,334	$ 12,334
DEATH BENEFIT YEAR 1	$ 94,816	$ 101,462	$ 160,915	$ 184,809
LTC POOL OF COVERAGE YEAR 1	$ 189,633	$ 202,924	$ 152,869	$ 175,569
MONTHLY LTC BENEFIT Year 1	$ 3,951	$ 4,228	$ 3,218	$ 3,696
DURATION OF BENEFIT (MONTHS)	$ 48	$ 48	$ 46	$ 46
LTC BENEFIT TYPE	INDEMNITY	REIMBURSEMENT	INDEMNITY	INDEMNITY
Elimination Period	90 days	90 days	90 Days	90 Days
Underwriting Method	Mortality and Morbidity	Mortality and Morbidity	Mortality only	Mortality only
Opportunity for growth of benefits	No	No	Yes	Yes
Trigger for claim	Loss of 2 of 6 ADL or cognitive impairment	Loss of 2 of 6 ADL or cognitive impairment	Loss of 2 of 6 ADL or cognitive impairment	Loss of 2 of 6 ADL or cognitive impairment
DEATH BENEFIT Year 10	$ 120,000	$ 101,462	$ 160,915	$ 184,809
POLICY SURRENDER VALUE Year 10	$ 72,723	$ 77,814	$ 79,046	$ 74,759
LTC POOL OF COVERAGE Year 10	$ 189,633	$ 202,924	$ 152,869	$ 175,569
DURATION OF BENEFIT (MONTHS)	$ 48	$ 48	$ 46	$ 46
DEATH BENEFIT Year 20	$ 120,000	$ 101,462	$ 160,915	$ 184,809
POLICY SURRENDER VALUE Year 20	$ 83,748	$ 88,605	$ 80,458	$ 92,405
LTC CARE POOL OF COVERAGE Year 20	$ 189,633	$ 202,924	$ 160,915	$ 184,809
DURATION OF BENEFIT (MONTHS)	$ 48	$ 48	$ 46	$ 46

These are just a couple of examples showing that each plan has its strengths and its weaknesses as compared to other plans. What features and benefits best suit your goals and objectives is what will drive your selection among the many choices. We like to explain this concept in this way…there are 100 cents in dollar. For all intents and purposes, most of the companies we work with operate similarly and have similar profit margins, expense loads, etc built into their coverage plans. So, in essence it is costing each of them about the same amount to do the whole job of multitasking benefits; the three main benefits being Long Term Care coverage, cash value accumulation that can be accessed during your lifetime and a death benefit that will ultimately be paid to your heirs.

If they all are operating on a 100-cent dollar, which they are, then anything they put toward one of those three main benefits will take away from the other two. If you want a higher death benefit, then you will have less cash value and less LTC benefits. If you want the highest LTC benefit, you will have less cash value and death benefit. It isn't rocket-science…it's just math. And this allows you to choose what pieces of this multitasking financial vehicle you want to be prioritized.

As an illustrative example, you can see the two choices on the right-hand side of the chart focus their weight on the death benefit component while ABC Company has the highest available pool of LTC benefits and XYZ company is sort of a middleman between the other two designs. Your specific goals and objectives will help determine the best course of action to take, but the winner will be determined later when we see if benefits were needed or not or if circumstances completely changed and coverage is no longer desired. In any of the choices noted above, you will have made a significant difference in your future for little to no cost to your overall planning.

Here is another example illustrating a similar but different offering…

Female (Nancy) -Widow

Born 1952, so she is 72 years old in 2024

Net Worth: Approximately $2,000,000

Retirement Plan Assets: $1,350,000

Liquid Assets: $250,000

Location: Massachusetts

Nancy has a well-diversified asset allocated investment portfolio which is designed to provide growth followed by income.

Using a lump sum, Nancy is setting aside $150,000 as a single payment to a HYBRID LTC/Life plan that leverages the premium deposit to provide living benefits, such as Long-Term Care (LTC) expense reimbursement. In this case, Nancy wanted to keep the design of the HYBRID product to primarily provide LTC benefits, if they are needed. Additionally, she wanted to provide some form of premium reimbursement if the LTC benefits are not needed or if only needed on a limited basis, meaning there were LTC benefits remaining unused in the plan.

As we described previously using the 100-cent dollar concept, there are three basic components we work with: cash value, death benefit and LTC benefits. The amount of weight applied to each of these components depends upon the product offerings and/or, in many cases, choices made by the insured when applying for the coverage.

People make choices in this regard based upon many factors, some of which include their interpretation of their own personal probability of needing LTC, their other assets earmarked for retirement income or perhaps to a planned legacy for their surviving family, the geographic location they reside in and how long before benefits are presumed to be needed and so on.

Intuitively, the LTC focus Nancy has chosen weights the premium to the Long-Term Care Benefit component much more so than in providing death benefit or cash value options for the plan. If Nancy chose to weight her components differently, it would reduce the LTC benefits she has available and increase the benefits in the other categories.

Nancy has a long life expectancy based upon her hereditary family history. Barring any unforeseen event, she expects to live into her 90's and understands that this assumption significantly increases the chances she will require long term custodial care. She has two children, but neither live near her nor will they be available for assisted living. Regardless, she does not want to burden her children with care, if needed, she would prefer to hire professional care.

She is looking to leverage some of her money to create a pool of benefits that she may need to use later in what Nancy assumes will likely be a long journey home…meaning she is likely to outlive normal life expectancy. She doesn't want to self-fund this risk by relying only on her existing investments. The leverage in a hybrid plan is significant and would be difficult to match in managing her $150,000 for use later. The leverage is too strong for her to match in a self-funding strategy without taking substantial risk to try and do so.

Nancy's worst-case, *guaranteed*, long-term scenario is that even if she *doesn't* use the pool of LTC benefits until year 25, her premiums earned the equivalent of over 5% for that 25-year period. If she uses the benefits earlier than that, the internal rate of return on her money is far greater. (See far right-hand column of exhibit 8 for internal rate of return equivalents when measuring the funds paid into the plan versus the benefit pool guaranteed in the plan in the years ahead)

This decision to utilize this HYBRID financial tool allows Nancy to think a little differently about how she comports herself in retirement. If she must constantly worry about the potential cost of LTC, she needs to be far more cautious with her invested portfolio of funds, even though that is contrary to what she would need to do if she were going to rely on her invested funds later to pay for LTC expenses out of pocket, also known as "Self -funding".

Exhibit 8.

Year	Age	Annual Premium	Surrender value	Death benefit	LONG-TERM CARE BENEFITS Inflation option: 3% compound			
					Total	Annual	Monthly	Internal Rate of Return (IRR)
1	71	$150,000	$76,629	$132,783	$277,757	$66,392	$5,533	41.77%
2	72	$0	$78,670	$132,783	$286,090	$68,383	$5,699	25.48%
3	73	$0	$80,730	$132,783	$294,673	$70,435	$5,870	19.01%
4	74	$0	$82,803	$132,783	$303,513	$72,548	$6,046	15.47%
5	75	$0	$84,884	$132,783	$312,618	$74,724	$6,227	13.22%
6	76	$0	$86,969	$132,783	$321,997	$76,966	$6,414	11.67%
7	77	$0	$89,052	$132,783	$331,657	$79,275	$6,606	10.53%
8	78	$0	$91,123	$132,783	$341,606	$81,653	$6,804	9.65%
9	79	$0	$93,168	$132,783	$351,855	$84,103	$7,009	8.96%
10	80	$0	$95,175	$132,783	$362,410	$86,626	$7,219	8.40%
11	81	$0	$97,150	$132,783	$373,283	$89,225	$7,435	7.93%
12	82	$0	$99,102	$132,783	$384,481	$91,901	$7,658	7.54%
13	83	$0	$101,025	$132,783	$396,015	$94,658	$7,888	7.21%
14	84	$0	$102,873	$132,783	$407,896	$97,498	$8,125	6.92%
15	85	$0	$104,633	$132,783	$420,133	$100,423	$8,369	6.67%
16	86	$0	$106,330	$132,783	$432,737	$103,436	$8,620	6.45%
17	87	$0	$107,955	$132,783	$445,719	$106,539	$8,878	6.25%
18	88	$0	$109,496	$132,783	$459,090	$109,735	$9,145	6.08%
19	89	$0	$110,951	$132,783	$472,863	$113,027	$9,419	5.92%
20	90	$0	$112,323	$132,783	$487,049	$116,418	$9,701	5.78%
21	91	$0	$113,616	$132,783	$501,660	$119,910	$9,993	5.65%
22	92	$0	$114,833	$132,783	$516,710	$123,508	$10,292	5.53%
23	93	$0	$115,987	$132,783	$532,212	$127,213	$10,601	5.43%
24	94	$0	$117,097	$132,783	$548,178	$131,029	$10,919	5.33%
25	95	$0	$118,150	$132,783	$564,623	$134,960	$11,247	5.24%
26	96	$0	$119,122	$132,783	$581,562	$139,009	$11,584	5.15%
27	97	$0	$120,005	$132,783	$599,009	$143,179	$11,932	5.08%
28	98	$0	$120,790	$132,783	$616,979	$147,475	$12,290	5.00%
29	99	$0	$121,461	$132,783	$635,489	$151,899	$12,658	4.94%
30	100	$0	$122,035	$132,783	$654,553	$156,456	$13,038	4.87%

Surrender value and death benefit columns reflect end-of-year values. Age and long-term care benefits reflect beginning-of-year values.

You can see in the chart provided what we mean when we talk about leverage. Nancy deposits $150,000 in this plan and IMMEDIATELY generates a pool of LTC benefits that is 185% of her premium deposit and it grows from there. At age 85, her $150,000 has been leveraged to $420,133. She would have had to earn about 6% *net after-tax* over 20+ years to equate to this pool of benefits at age 85. Her money is not sitting idle throughout the years.

◊ Benefits such as the LTC expense reimbursement as well as any life insurance benefits paid from these plans is generally income tax free. If she were to take her funds from her retirement account(s), she would have to account for income taxes which means she would have to use even that much more of her money to provide the same dollars available for LTC expenses.

◊ As an example, $420,133 of LTC benefits at age 85 would require Nancy to withdraw about $560,000 before tax to have the same $420,000 to cover expenses. (Assumes a 25% tax bracket)

◊ Let's look at how you can customize, to some degree, various plan designs to best meet your own particular goals and objectives in considering a plan that will help mitigate Long Term Care expenses.

Exhibit 9.

LTC benefit period	Inflation option	Face amount	Day 1: maximum LTC monthly benefit	Day 1: total LTC benefit	Age 85: maximum LTC monthly benefit	Age 85: total LTC benefit	Total LTC crossover age[12]
4 years	None	$172,442	$7,185	$344,884	$7,185	$344,884	N/A
4 years	3% Simple	$136,123	$5,672	$284,497	$8,054	$398,840	79
4 years	3% Compound	$132,783	$5,533	$277,757	$8,369	$420,133	79
4 years	5% Simple	$120,142	$5,006	$258,305	$8,510	$426,504	79
4 years	5% Compound	$88,786	$3,699	$191,340	$7,325	$378,839	84
5 years	None	$164,980	$6,874	$412,450	$6,874	$412,450	N/A
5 years	3% Simple	$128,851	$5,369	$341,456	$7,624	$476,749	79
5 years	3% Compound	$125,501	$5,229	$333,152	$7,910	$503,922	79
5 years	5% Simple	$113,194	$4,716	$311,284	$8,018	$509,373	79
5 years	5% Compound	$82,734	$3,447	$228,579	$6,825	$452,570	84
6 years	None	$160,497	$6,687	$481,491	$6,687	$481,491	N/A
6 years	3% Simple	$124,514	$5,188	$401,558	$7,367	$558,445	79
6 years	3% Compound	$121,152	$5,048	$391,830	$7,636	$592,679	78
6 years	5% Simple	$109,070	$4,545	$368,111	$7,726	$597,158	78
6 years	5% Compound	$79,150	$3,298	$269,186	$6,530	$532,969	83
7 years	None	$152,671	$6,361	$534,349	$6,361	$534,349	N/A
7 years	3% Simple	$115,203	$4,800	$439,500	$6,816	$608,849	79
7 years	3% Compound	$111,759	$4,657	$428,175	$7,044	$647,653	79
7 years	5% Simple	$99,743	$4,156	$401,466	$7,065	$645,837	79
7 years	5% Compound	$70,680	$2,945	$287,739	$5,831	$569,703	84
8 years	None	$147,314	$6,138	$589,256	$6,138	$589,256	N/A
8 years	3% Simple	$109,067	$4,544	$482,076	$6,453	$665,309	80
8 years	3% Compound	$105,605	$4,400	$469,538	$6,656	$710,218	79
8 years	5% Simple	$93,702	$3,904	$440,400	$6,637	$702,765	79
8 years	5% Compound	$65,409	$2,725	$312,299	$5,396	$618,330	85

There are many design choices that influence the various benefits available, but for purposes of this discussion, we are simply showing you if Nancy wanted a more balanced approach for her HYBRID plan, she can choose to do so at the onset of the plan.

Other variables and choices factor into plan design. This is something you should discuss with your Financial Sherpa. Some important considerations include the benefit *period* covered (2 years, 3 years, 4 years, 5 years and so on) and the *method and amount for calculating inflation benefits* (3% or 5% compounding or simple-or NO inflation benefits at all).

David likes to remind folks that *"no decision is a decision unto itself"* as he ponders a situation from his past when he strongly suggested a similar LTC solution to a client of his in New Hampshire. Dave felt so strongly about his recommendation for this client that he had the husband sign a letter that he was choosing, on his own, to forgo the recommendation Dave had made.

Low and behold, several years later the couple found themselves in need of care for the wife and ended up paying out of pocket several hundreds of thousands of dollars for her necessary care. The husband was upset thinking back upon their journey as to why nobody had ever talked to him about this risk. The financial assets he had to use for her care now left him without sufficient assets to produce the ongoing income he needed. He called David and was quite upset that David had not told him to take care of this risk. While David had empathy for the situation, he promptly pulled his letter from the file and showed the husband that he did, in fact, extensively discuss the idea of insuring against this very thing and the husband had opted out of that idea thinking it would cost too much money. The indecision was a decision in itself and, unfortunately, ended up being quite a costly one. For some very small adjustments to their situation when the planning was in early stages, they could have avoided this entire catastrophe.

Let's look at one more example…

Married couple

Jack-age 59

Diane-age 53

3 adult aged children

Total Assets: $3,850,000

Retirement Plan assets: $1,680,000

Liquid cash equivalents: $365,000

Objective: Reposition $200,000 of liquid assets to provide some leverage for potential long-term care benefits of either spouse.

In the case of Jack and Diane, a HYBRID LTC ANNUITY was their choice of preference among many options. Here too, there are plan design choices that can be made such as whether to include inflation protection benefits or enhanced cash surrender values. Neither of these two choices was elected by Jack and Diane. They opted for a simple plan design and anticipate growth on their money within the plan to increase future benefits as compared to the initial benefits created at time of policy issue.

Exhibit 10.

HYBRID LTC ANNUITY

Age(s)	Guaranteed Interest Rate	Interest Earned	LTC Charge	Death Benefit	Cash Value	LTC Benefit Pool	Maximum Monthly Benefit	LTC Benefit Period "per spouse" (Months)
59 / 53	6.00%	$ 11,934	$ 2,061	$ 209,873	$ 194,683	$ 629,619	$ 6,996	90.0
60 / 54	1.00%	$ 2,087	$ 2,116	$ 209,873	$ 194,752	$ 629,619	$ 6,996	90.0
61 / 55	1.00%	$ 2,087	$ 2,116	$ 209,873	$ 196,651	$ 629,619	$ 6,996	90.0
62 / 56	1.00%	$ 2,087	$ 2,116	$ 209,873	$ 198,540	$ 629,619	$ 6,996	90.0
63 / 57	1.00%	$ 2,087	$ 2,116	$ 209,873	$ 200,429	$ 629,619	$ 6,996	90.0
64 / 58	1.00%	$ 2,087	$ 2,116	$ 209,873	$ 202,317	$ 629,619	$ 6,996	90.0
65 / 59	1.00%	$ 2,087	$ 2,116	$ 209,873	$ 204,206	$ 629,619	$ 6,996	90.0
66 / 60	1.00%	$ 2,087	$ 2,116	$ 209,873	$ 206,095	$ 629,619	$ 6,996	90.0
67 / 61	1.00%	$ 2,087	$ 2,116	$ 209,873	$ 207,984	$ 629,619	$ 6,996	90.0
68 /62	0.10%	$ 210	$ 2,116	$ 209,873	$ 212,973	$ 629,619	$ 6,996	90.0
69 / 63	0.10%	$ 210	$ 2,116	$ 209,873	$ 218,973	$ 629,619	$ 6,996	90.0
70 / 64	0.10%	$ 210	$ 2,116	$ 209,873	$ 225,324	$ 629,619	$ 6,996	90.0
71 / 65	0.10%	$ 210	$ 2,116	$ 209,873	$ 231,866	$ 629,619	$ 6,996	90.0
72 / 66	0.10%	$ 210	$ 2,116	$ 209,873	$ 238,604	$ 629,619	$ 6,996	90.0
73 / 67	0.10%	$ 210	$ 2,116	$ 209,873	$ 245,545	$ 629,619	$ 6,996	90.0
74 / 68	0.10%	$ 210	$ 2,116	$ 209,873	$ 252,693	$ 629,619	$ 6,996	90.0
75 /69	0.10%	$ 210	$ 2,116	$ 209,873	$ 260,056	$ 629,619	$ 6,996	90.0
76 / 70	0.10%	$ 210	$ 2,116	$ 209,873	$ 267,640	$ 629,619	$ 6,996	90.0
77 / 71	0.10%	$ 210	$ 2,116	$ 209,873	$ 275,452	$ 629,619	$ 6,996	90.0
78 / 72	0.10%	$ 210	$ 2,116	$ 209,873	$ 283,497	$ 629,619	$ 6,996	90.0

As you can see in Exhibit 10, the single lump sum deposit of $200,000 created an immediate pool of benefits equal to 3 X the Death Benefit of the Annuity for Jack and Diane. If the Death Benefit grows based upon interest rates in excess of the guarantees, the benefit pool coincidentally increases as well.

Exhibit 10 reflects contractually guaranteed interest rates.

Exhibit 11 reflects non-guaranteed current rates for all future years to remain unchanged from the year 1 guarantee rate of 6%. While we certainly don't expect that this 6% rate will be paid in each year of the policy going forward, we do anticipate the crediting rate to be more than the guarantees shown in Exhibit 10. Actual interest rate credit will adjust as interest rates change in general. Non-guaranteed crediting rates are declared annually.

In this example for Jack and Diane, we view Exhibit 10 as the worst-case scenario and Exhibit 11 as best-case scenario. We anticipate reality will fall somewhere in between these two iterations.

Exhibit 11.

Age(s)	CURRENT Interest Rate	Interest Earned	LTC Charge	Death Benefit	Cash Value	LTC Benefit Pool	Maximum Monthly Benefit	LTC Benefit Period "per spouse" (Months)
59 / 53	6.00%	$ 11,934	$ 2,061	$ 209,873	$ 194,683	$ 629,619	$ 6,996	90.0
60 / 54	6.00%	$ 12,523	$ 2,163	$ 220,233	$ 204,293	$ 660,699	$ 7,341	90.0
61 / 55	6.00%	$ 13,141	$ 2,270	$ 231,105	$ 216,469	$ 693,315	$ 7,704	90.0
62 / 56	6.00%	$ 13,790	$ 2,362	$ 242,513	$ 229,349	$ 727,539	$ 8,084	90.0
63 / 57	6.00%	$ 14,475	$ 2,499	$ 254,485	$ 242,973	$ 763,455	$ 8,483	90.0
64 / 58	6.00%	$ 15,185	$ 2,623	$ 267,047	$ 257,383	$ 801,141	$ 8,902	90.0
65 / 59	6.00%	$ 15,935	$ 2,752	$ 280,230	$ 272,624	$ 840,690	$ 9,341	90.0
66 / 60	6.00%	$ 16,721	$ 2,888	$ 294,063	$ 288,742	$ 882,189	$ 9,802	90.0
67 / 61	6.00%	$ 17,547	$ 3,031	$ 308,579	$ 305,788	$ 925,737	$ 10,286	90.0
68 /62	6.00%	$ 18,443	$ 3,180	$ 323,812	$ 323,812	$ 971,436	$ 10,794	90.0
69 / 63	6.00%	$ 19,322	$ 3,337	$ 339,797	$ 339,797	$ 1,019,391	$ 11,327	90.0
70 / 64	6.00%	$ 20,276	$ 3,502	$ 356,571	$ 356,571	$ 1,069,713	$ 11,886	90.0
71 / 65	6.00%	$ 21,277	$ 3,675	$ 374,173	$ 374,173	$ 1,122,519	$ 12,472	90.0
72 / 66	6.00%	$ 22,327	$ 3,856	$ 392,644	$ 392,644	$ 1,177,932	$ 13,088	90.0
73 / 67	6.00%	$ 23,429	$ 4,047	$ 412,026	$ 412,026	$ 1,236,078	$ 13,734	90.0
74 / 68	6.00%	$ 24,586	$ 4,246	$ 432,366	$ 432,366	$ 1,297,098	$ 14,412	90.0
75 /69	6.00%	$ 25,799	$ 4,456	$ 453,709	$ 453,709	$ 1,361,127	$ 15,124	90.0
76 / 70	6.00%	$ 27,073	$ 4,675	$ 476,106	$ 476,106	$ 1,428,318	$ 15,870	90.0
77 / 71	6.00%	$ 28,440	$ 4,907	$ 499,609	$ 499,609	$ 1,498,827	$ 16,654	90.0
78 / 72	6.00%	$ 29,812	$ 5,149	$ 524,272	$ 524,272	$ 1,572,816	$ 17,476	90.0

HYBRID LTC ANNUITY

As shown in Exhibit 11, as the values on the left-hand side of the contract are increasing, so too is the joint pool of LTC benefits available to each spouse. The maximum monthly benefit is available for each spouse but is limited overall by the total LTC Benefit Pool.

To be sure you are tracking these exhibits correctly, Exhibit 11 reflects that the death benefit of the policy grew from $209,873 in year 1 to $534,272 in year 20, assuming 6% interest. Since the overall LTC pool of benefits is a function of the death benefit, 3 X the Death Benefit in year 20 = $1,572,816. To determine the maximum monthly benefit, you simply divide the total pool of available benefits by the number of months noted as maximum benefit period. In this case, $1,572,816 divided by 90 months = a maximum monthly benefit of $17,476. Note that each spouse can claim eligible benefits up to that maximum, but Jack and Diane's joint claims cannot exceed the total LTC pool.

It is worth noting here that if claims are made that do *not* reach the maximum monthly benefit amount, leaving unused benefits, those unused benefits will extend the benefit period beyond 90 months. As an example, if total monthly benefits eligible for reimbursement are $10,000 per month in year 20 and the maximum monthly benefit available equals that shown in Exhibit 11, $17,476 then the difference in those amounts can extend the pool of benefits beyond the initial maximum of 90 months.

So, now you have seen 5 different LTC solutions. Each brings its own special set of features and benefits. By clearly understanding your goals and objectives as they relate to the potential risk of needing Long Term Care, together we can design a plan that will serve you best.

What have we learned or confirmed here?

1. Long Term Care costs are likely the most significant risk hanging over your retirement plan
2. Without proper planning, even just one spouse's long term care event can be a road hazard that cannot be overcome financially by a married couple
3. There are a multitude of plans available today, each with its own special design features and benefits. Which one is best suited for your situation depends upon many factors including your ultimate goals and objectives in managing risk
4. Many of the plans today multitask, meaning they have benefits for many situations and allow flexibility to avoid being stuck should circumstances change in the future
5. Properly insuring against a potential LTC event is likely best done by leveraging funds you have available today. Self-insuring does nothing to avoid exposure to a possible event of this magnitude. You really can't save your way out if care is needed for any extended period of time
6. The younger and healthier you are when you consider this risk, the more options you will have to choose from

CHAPTER SIX

MONTE CARLO...NOT THE CASINO IN MONACO

While investing in the stock market might feel like a trip to the casino at times, the Monte Carlo we want to discuss today is something that does help predict odds/probabilities, just not the ones for use at the blackjack table.

In the financial/investment world, there is something used to help predict future outcomes called a Monte Carlo Simulation. Monte Carlo simulations are a way to model probability of outcomes in a world where there are many variables. It helps us understand risk and uncertainty as it relates to the potential outcomes for a retirement portfolio.

Monte Carlo simulation assesses risk using multiple random input values and averaging results. In our world, they are used to predict the probability of success (not outliving your money) over the course of a period. In a more specific description for us, a Monte Carlo Simulation takes thousands and thousands of randomly generated inputs to generate probability of outcomes to evaluate what rate of distribution someone can use from their retirement plan assets without the risk of running out of money. We will call this a safe money rate. (Safety)

As you can imagine, the higher the rate of distribution from an asset, all else being the same, the faster the funds will run out. Also intuitive to this equation, the higher the rate of return on invested funds is projected to be, the higher the projected distribution rate can be without impacting the long-term outcome.

Remembering what we said in Chapter 3 about the risk of using *average* rates of returns in forecasting, the Monte Carlo simulation is intended to help us avoid drowning in that water that is *averaging* six inches deep.

Running thousands of random inputs, Monte Carlo can help us account for varying market conditions, interest rate fluctuations and inflation...helping us determine as realistic and sound a projection for a safe money distribution rate as we can find.

In reviewing Exhibit 12, you can see how this type of analysis can help us choose a safe money distribution rate. This chart illustrates that the lower the distribution rate, the higher the probability of success (success defined as not running out of money before we meet our demise).

Let's start by looking at the 3% distribution rate (dark blue line at top of graph) there is almost 100% probability of our money lasting to age 100(35 years), assuming we are age 65 today. If we increase the distribution rate to the other extreme in this chart, at 8% (orange line), we have almost no chance of being successful with a nearly 0% probability of retirement funds lasting to age 100. In fact, at an 8% distribution rate, the portfolio only has a 10% probability of lasting 25 years and 60% probability of lasting 15 years.

Exhibit 12

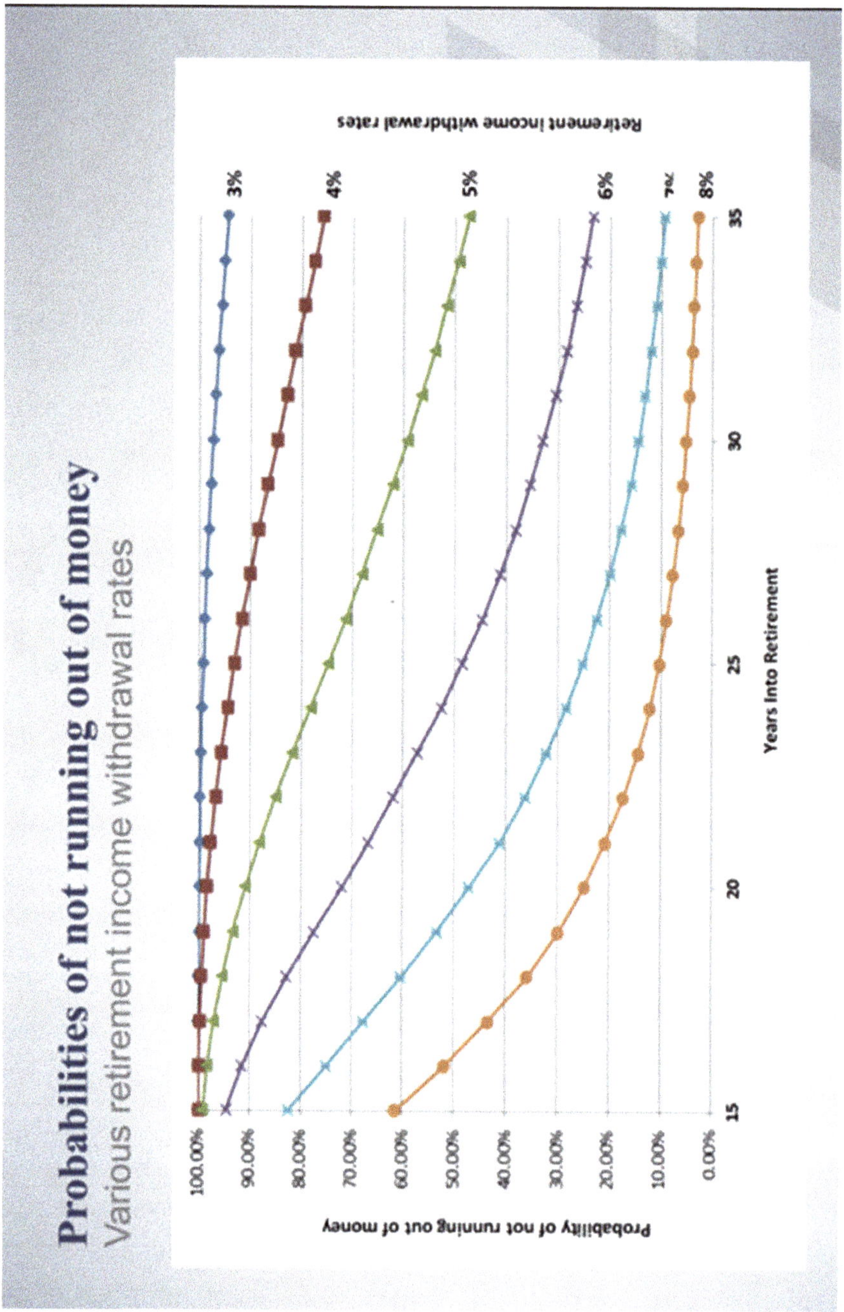
Probabilities of not running out of money
Various retirement income withdrawal rates
Probability of not running out of money
100.00%
90.00%
80.00%
70.00%
60.00%
50.00%
40.00%
30.00%
20.00%
10.00%
0.00%
15
20
25
30
35
Years Into Retirement
3%
4%
5%
6%
7%
8%
Retirement income withdrawal rates

Now, at this point some of you may be sitting looking at a chart like this, and interpreting for yourself that based upon what you need for income during retirement and the projection of what you will have already packed in your rucksack for the trip in terms of supplies, that you can or will need to accept a lower probability of success in order to meet the distribution rate you need. As was mentioned in previous chapters, most folks are not going to be satisfied working with a 3% rate of distribution as it is not likely to meet their income needs or wants during retirement. It can be a dangerous game, however, to plan to simply take your chances and opt to try and beat the odds. We all know how that usually goes at the casino.

If you were boarding a plane tomorrow and the airline announced that there is a 60% probability of making it safely to the intended destination, would you fly? It is highly unlikely you will board that plane. Similarly, you shouldn't be navigating your way down the mountain so quickly that it is most probable you will not make the journey safely.

When the analysis of what you need for income contrasts with the computational results as shown in exhibit 12, this is where you should be contemplating the distribution power of incorporating strategies that include volatility buffers(assets not correlated to market) as discussed in chapter 4, as well as use of actuarially science based solutions, thereby allowing you to more safely increase your distribution rate.

Exhibit 13

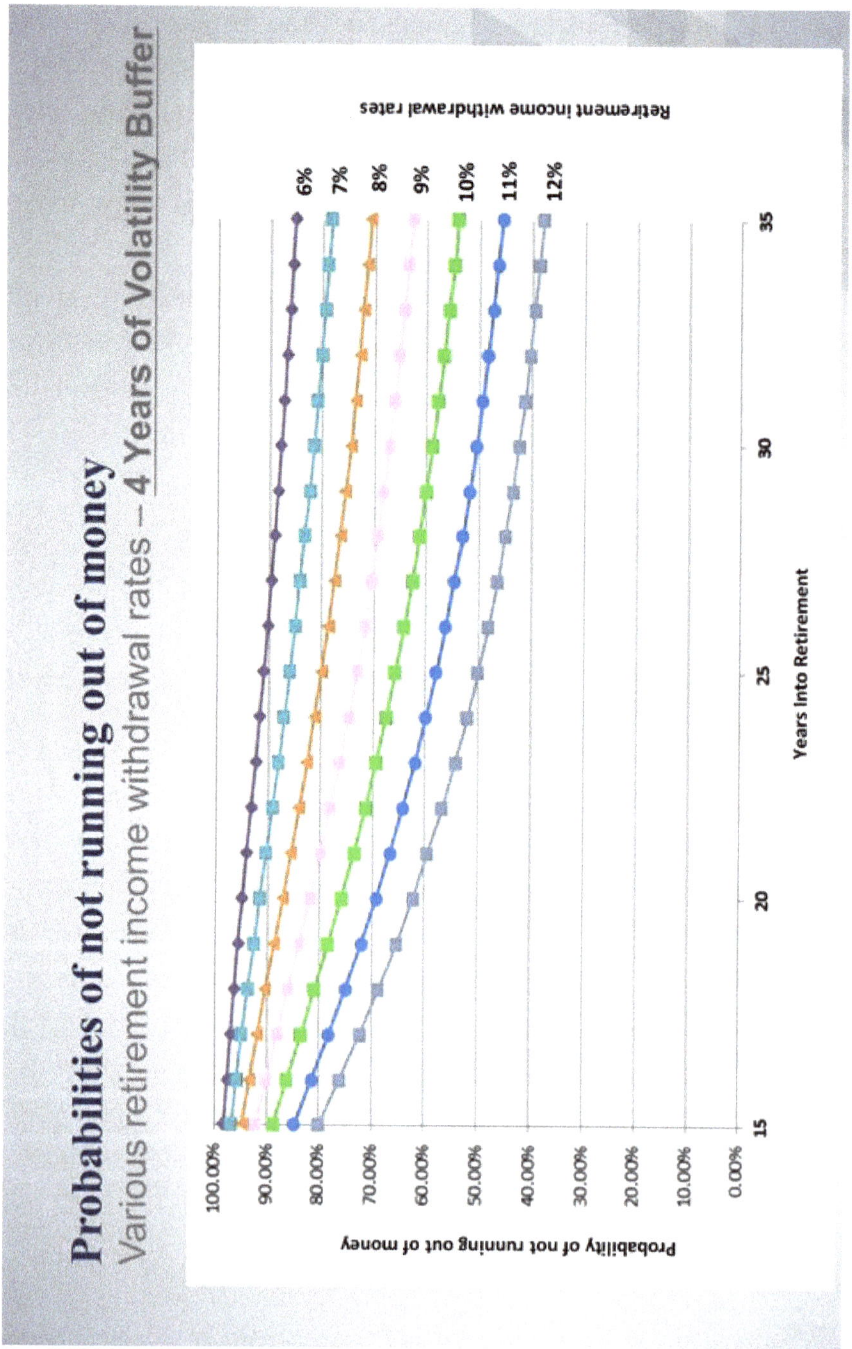
Probabilities of not running out of money
Various retirement income withdrawal rates – 4 Years of Volatility Buffer
Probability of not running out of money
100.00%
90.00%
80.00%
70.00%
60.00%
50.00%
40.00%
30.00%
20.00%
10.00%
0.00%
15
20
25
30
35
Years Into Retirement
Retirement income withdrawal rates
6%
7%
8%
9%
10%
11%
12%

In exhibit 13, as compared to Exhibit 12, we can clearly see that by adding a volatility buffer to your overall plan you have added significant power to the equation in terms of probability of success.

As a quick example and to help you follow along, in exhibit 12, a 6% distribution rate had just about a 20% probability of success. With a volatility buffer sufficient to cover up to 4 years of retirement income, using the same 6% distribution rate, the probability of success has improved to almost 90%.

And, as seen in Exhibit 14, by having an even larger non-correlated bucket, in this example up to 7 years' worth of income, the probability of success at a 6% distribution rate has crept up over 90% and actually indicates you may be able to consider even a 7% distribution rate without losing any ground in terms of success probability.

Exhibit 14

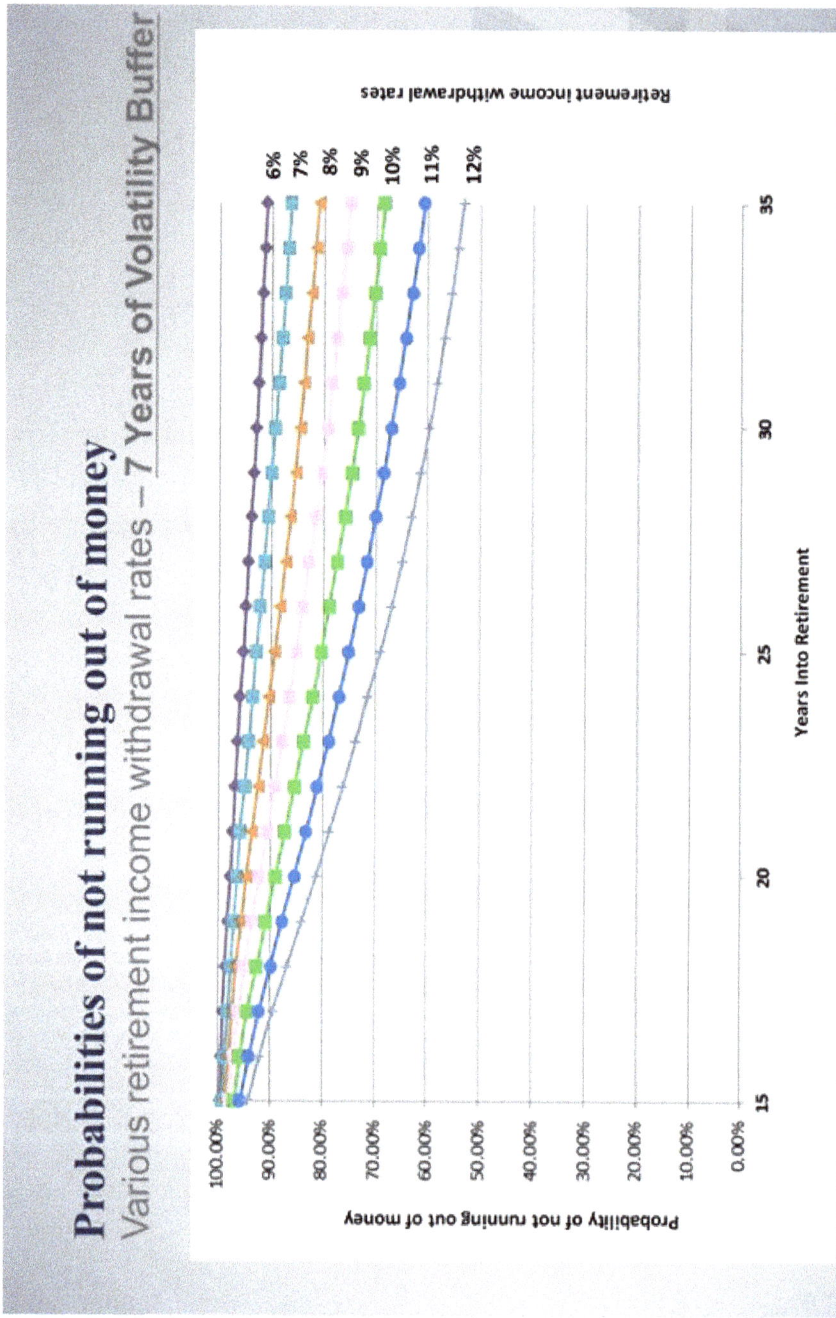
Probabilities of not running out of money
Various retirement income withdrawal rates – 7 Years of Volatility Buffer
Probability of not running out of money
100.00%
90.00%
80.00%
70.00%
60.00%
50.00%
40.00%
30.00%
20.00%
10.00%
0.00%
15
20
25
30
35
Years Into Retirement
6%
7%
8%
9%
10%
11%
12%
Retirement income withdrawal rates

As of the writing of this book, that safe distribution rate hovers around 3% without incorporating strategic plans to provide more certainty. Over the past 40 years, we've seen that number at 4% and we've seen more conservative results below 3%. The implication is that a distribution of $30,000 can be taken annually from a $1,000,000 asset invested in an appropriately diversified portfolio delivering perhaps a 95% probability that the funds will last for the next 25-30 years.

The aforementioned conundrum still looms large, however. Nobody who has $1,000,000 as their nest egg can survive on $30,000 annually as their retirement income, even when coupled with other sources such as social security.

In referring back to some of our prior chapters, we showed you an example of someone taking $50,000 from a $1,000,000 asset. That equates to a 5% distribution rate. Due to market volatility, this path was not sustainable for the long term. One way to have handled that issue would have been to adhere to a rate closer to the 3% Monte Carlo safe money rate. While that might not have completely cured this situation, it clearly would have meant there would be more money remaining at the end of the period being measured.

However, as we also stated previously, living on $30,000 from a $1,000,000 asset is not a doable situation for most people that we work with. So, your next natural question is going to be "how can I increase my safe distribution rate without increasing the chances of incurring risk that I really don't want to take?"

Sherpa Dave considering choices with his clients

Decisions like this are just the reason you should seek the insight of a financial sherpa. Your decisions are going to require balancing risk and reward and a good sherpa will be cognizant of and a good reminder of the potential risks and have access to viable solutions that can deliver enough reward to meet the balance required for such considerations.

What did we learn or confirm here?

1. There are methods available today to gauge a safe money rate of distribution for retirement income planning-you don't need to shoot in the dark
2. While we can estimate a workable safe money rate, there is no crystal ball for the future and events may come along that will require adjustments to your plan for future years
3. Monte Carlo method incorporates market volatility into the equation helping avoid the pitfalls of projecting constant average returns.
4. Strategic use of non-correlated assets can significantly improve your safe distribution rate

CHAPTER SEVEN

NOT YOUR GRANDDAD'S PENSION

This seems like a good time to remind ourselves how we got here and why we have all of this "stuff" to consider when contemplating and planning our trip back to base camp.

The landscape has shifted. Your grandfather was quite likely a participant in what we refer to as a pension plan. These were defined "benefit" plans that provided predetermined monthly retirement income benefits based upon a stated formula, typically using years of service multiplied by an earnings definition such as average of the highest three years, or something similar. The formula would produce a maximum monthly benefit payable to the retiree for their lifetime. Adjustments to this maximum pension benefit would be made to offset any cost of insuring a continuing income to a surviving spouse. The more that was also guaranteed to the spouse, the higher the deduction would be from the maximum benefit.

As an example; Grandpa worked for 35 years at XYZ company. The pension that his company provided included a formula that used an average of his last three years of income. His average income was $55,000. The formula provided for 35 years X 55 = 1,925 or $1,925 per month in maximum pension income.

If he wanted to continue 100% of his pension to his spouse upon his death, the cost to do so might have been 20%. So, $1,925 X 20% = $385. This would mean both he, and subsequently his wife if he predeceases her, will receive $1,540 per month guaranteed for their respective lifetimes. ($1,925 - $385 = $1,540)

(the numbers above are for discussion and illustrative purposes only. They do not represent an actual pension recipient)

The point is your grandfather knew what his retirement would be based upon a pre-determined formula, and he retired counting on that pension plan sending him his retirement check every month no matter what the stock market was doing or what prevailing interest rates were or any other economic or financial occurrence that might otherwise impact monetary results. He knew the route to base camp that provided a strong track record of success at a reasonable and acceptable pace.

The promise of a viable retirement income coupled with social security and perhaps with a nice gold watch to ice the cake was a simpler time in our history, a time when there seemed to be a lot less peril to consider and much more certainty in life. Grandpa didn't have to manage his route to base camp as we must do today because the hazards such as investment risk and interest rate risk were risks the employer had to worry about, not him, and some of the other obstacles we have to consider today were not even there at all when he was descending the trail. Additionally, life expectancy was shorter and planning for retirement did not typically include needing to worry about longevity related issues.

Times have changed for sure. Retirees today are far more responsible for creating, funding and maintaining their own respective retirement plans.

Historically, here are some milestone dates and changes in the retirement plan marketplace…

◊ 1974 - Employee Retirement Income Security Act of 1974. ERISA

◊ 1978 - Introduction of the 401(K)

◊ 1981- IRS makes a ruling to allow payroll deductions for employee contributions to their 401(K)

◊ 1983- there were 7.1 million employees participating in 401(k)

◊ 1993- employee participation in 401(k) had risen to 38.7 million people

◊ 2001-The Economic Growth and Tax Relief Reconciliation Act (EGTRRA) provided for catch up contributions for employees over age 50. Also provided for increased contribution limit for IRA's and other retirement vehicles.

◊ 2006- introduction of the ROTH 401(k) -allowing employees to elect *after-tax* contributions into their 401(k).

◊ 2006-Introduction of the Pension Protection Act (See below for more detailed information on this ACT) Up to this date this was the largest, most impactful retirement plan act for retirement plan reform.

◊ 2015- Protecting Americans from Tax Hikes (PATH) Act-allows for direct and favorable treatment of *charitable* contributions from Traditional IRA and ROTH IRA.

◊ 2019- Introduction of the Setting Every Community Up for Retirement Enhancement (Secure Act 1.0, enacted January 1, 2020) Major change for non-spousal beneficiaries, requiring a 10-year rule for accepting inherited retirement plan monies which previously allowed these monies to be stretched over the beneficiary's lifetime. (Please see our chapter on Inherited IRA's)

◊ 2022- The SECURE ACT 2.0 (Some provisions of this ACT are in effect as of January 1, 2023 while others will go into effect in 2024 and 2025 and beyond.) The most notable change reflects the increased age to begin required minimum distributions which is currently Age 73 for some and up to age 75 for others beginning in 2033.

◊ 2023- approximately 60 million active participants and about 110 million people overall with 401(k) assets. This means approximately 1/3 of US residents are currently participants with assets in a 401(k) plan.

Grandpa's Pension Plan was not without risk, however, even though it provided a significant amount of certainty beyond that which is available today in defined contribution plans.

As you will see in the next chapter, congress got involved to try and provide some guardrails and road rules to alleviate this uncertainty.

What did we learn or confirm here?

1. Most retirement plans today are defined contribution plans and require the employee to make good decisions that will shape the outlook for their retirement

2. The majority of employer sponsored retirement plans today are 401(k) plans

3. The landscape for retirement savings programs is ever shifting in terms of the rules, regulations and offerings that are available

CHAPTER EIGHT

I'M FROM THE GOVERNMENT AND I AM HERE TO HELP

Please keep in mind that while most Congressional Acts related to Pension and Retirement plans are designed to improve the retirement planning landscape for employees, in many cases the ACTS have caused confusion and indecision as folks try and figure out how to navigate constantly changing rules and regulations.

Pension Protection Act

The Pension Protection Act, enacted in 2006, was designed to strengthen the financial health of pension plans in the United States and provide greater security for retirees who depend on them. Here's how it impacts retirees:

1. Improved Funding for Pension Plans: The Act requires companies to fully fund their defined benefit pension plans over a seven-year period. This ensures that the plans have enough

assets to cover future obligations, providing more security for retirees.

2. Enhanced Disclosure and Transparency: Companies must regularly disclose the funding status of their pension plans. This transparency allows retirees to better understand the health of their pension and make informed financial decisions.

3. Restrictions on Underfunded Plans: To protect retirees, the Act imposes restrictions on underfunded plans, such as limiting lump-sum payouts and benefit increases until the plan's financial status improves.

4. Protection for Beneficiaries: The Act includes provisions to ensure that surviving spouses receive adequate benefits.

Overall, the Pension Protection Act aims to protect retirees by ensuring that pension plans are adequately funded and transparent, providing peace of mind about their financial security in retirement.

The Pension Protection Act (PPA) brought about changes that impact how beneficiaries receive retirement plan benefits:

1. Survivor Benefits: The Act reinforced protections for spouses by ensuring that defined benefit plans and certain defined contribution plans offer a qualified joint and survivor annuity. This means that surviving spouses are more likely to receive continued benefits after the participant's death.

2. Automatic Enrollment: The PPA encouraged automatic enrollment in 401(k) and other defined contribution plans, which can lead to increased participation and savings. This indirectly benefits beneficiaries by potentially increasing the retirement savings available for distribution.

3. Non-Spouse Beneficiaries: Before the PPA, non-spouse beneficiaries did not have the same flexibility in rolling over inherited plan assets. The Act allowed non-spouse beneficiaries to roll over inherited assets into an inherited Individual Retirement Account (IRA), thereby enabling better tax management and planning for inherited assets.

These changes were designed to provide more options and security for beneficiaries, ensuring that they receive the benefits in a manner that aligns with their financial needs and circumstances.

The SECURE act 1.0 (2019)

The Setting Every Community Up for Retirement Enhancement (SECURE) Act, enacted in December 2019, is legislation aimed at improving the retirement savings landscape in the United States beyond that which is provided in the Pension Protection Act. Here are some key aspects of the SECURE Act and how it impacts retirement planning:

1. Increased Access to Retirement Plans: The SECURE Act makes it easier for small businesses to offer retirement plans by allowing them to join together to offer Multiple Employer Plans (MEPs), which can help reduce administrative costs.

2. Repeal of Maximum Age for Traditional IRA Contributions: Previously, individuals could not contribute to a traditional Individual Retirement Account (IRA) after age 70½. The SECURE Act removed this age limit, allowing contributions at any age as long as the individual has earned income.

3. Raising the Required Minimum Distribution (RMD) Age: The Act increased the age at which individuals must start taking RMDs from their retirement accounts from 70½ to 72, allowing more time for retirement savings to grow.

4. ***This Required Minimum Distribution start date is now age 73 and will be age 75 by 2033.***

5. Lifetime Income Options: The SECURE Act encourages the inclusion of lifetime income options, like annuities, in retirement plans, providing opportunities for retirees to receive a steady income stream in retirement.

6. Beneficiary Distribution Rules: It altered the rules for non-spousal beneficiaries, requiring most beneficiaries to withdraw inherited retirement plan assets within ten years, commonly known as the "10-year rule."

The SECURE Act aims to enhance retirement security by expanding access to retirement plans, providing more flexibility in saving and withdrawing retirement funds, and encouraging lifetime income strategies.

The SECURE Act 2.0,

Proposed to build upon the changes made by the initial legislation. Here's a brief overview of each:

1. SECURE Act of 2019: This is the original version signed into law in December 2019. It includes provisions like increasing the Required Minimum Distribution (RMD) age, eliminating the maximum age for traditional IRA contributions, and promoting access to retirement plans through Multiple Employer Plans (MEPs).

2. SECURE Act 2.0: This legislation seeks to further enhance retirement savings and financial security. It includes potential changes such as further increasing the RMD age (from 72 to 75), increasing catch-up contribution limits for older

workers, and simplifying some retirement plan rules for both individuals and plan sponsors.

The aim of both versions is to provide greater flexibility, security, and opportunities for individuals to save for retirement, reflecting ongoing efforts to adapt to the evolving needs of retirees.

While many of today's plans still include corporate contributions in the form of profit sharing and/or matching contributions, the onus is now on the employee to be sure their retirement plan will meet their objectives.

The employee is now responsible for determining contribution levels sufficient to meet long-term savings goals and they will be required to make their own investment decisions based on their risk tolerance and the time horizon for their planned arrival at the summit. There will be traditional vs. ROTH decisions to consider and ultimately, decisions as to how the resources that have been accumulated will be deployed...how to provide the maximum sustainable income in the most tax efficient manner, while making sure there is sufficient liquidity to meet unexpected times along the way and also have reserves for major financial risks such as long-term care expenses.

There are pros and cons to this change in landscape. Some will say people are better off fending for themselves, so to speak, rather than relying on a company sponsored pension plan.

Defined contribution plans provide more flexibility for employees than defined benefit plans. Perhaps the investment results achieved are better than the more conservatively managed defined benefit plan assets may have been. And let's face it, it is rare today that someone is working for the same company for years on end. People are much more mobile today. Formulas that rely on years of service are not favorable. Having plans that can move with the employee makes sense.

There is far less certainty for retirees in today's landscape and a far more complicated world to be navigated.

Improvements in longevity have changed everything. People are living much longer and so the period for which we must worry about funding for our retirement is much different than Grandpa had to consider. Planning for the changes that will occur over 30 years is far different than planning for the next 15 years. And plain as day, the most obvious difference is personal health. The cost of health care outpaces inflation, the cost of long-term custodial care outpaces inflation and the need for this medical care and/or custodial intervention is imminent with life expectancies approaching the mid-eighties and beyond.

We are the ones who are now tasked with making the right choices for investments, managing risk, generating adequate and sustainable income while simultaneously keeping up with inflation, all complicated by longer life expectancy that typically results in increased medical costs and exorbitant long-term custodial care expenses.

We need to pack a new bag, replace some old straps and be sure we are taking up-to-date ideas and resources with us for our journey. While we need the wisdom of experience, we also need the contemporary tools and techniques born from that experience.

The route Grandpa took isn't open any longer.

What did we learn or confirm here?

1. The government has enacted many changes to broaden and simplify the retirement plan landscape

2. New regulations seem to try and better reflect demographic changes such as extending the required minimum distribution date
3. Some guidelines are helpful and others are more restrictive
4. How current and new regulations will impact retirement is something worth paying attention to. What works best or what might be available to one person may be very different for someone else.

CHAPTER NINE

SOCIAL SECURITY

You are approaching the summit and before you can even enjoy the achievement, you have several considerations to make about the alternative routes ahead for your descent. Who will be descending with you? Are they strong enough to finish the journey with you? What supplies are *they* bringing to the table in addition to your own? Should you utilize support resources and expedite your journey or save the resources for a potentially prolonged descent?

These are just a few of the considerations we must consider as we approach the Summit. Is it just one of us making this journey or are two of us working together? Are we prepared to make decisions for the best of the pair or are we focused on our own survival only? What is the likelihood of both of us having a prolonged journey down? Are we better to enjoy some resources now and improve our descent early on or should we reserve everything for the benefit of the potentially long road ahead?

Just as it is on the mountain, answering these questions provides structure to our decision making as we consider when and how to employ our social security retirement income benefits, but the reality is that we have no idea what may come our way. We are relegated to making the best decisions today that we can make with the knowledge and information we have at our disposal, while fully understanding that there are variables beyond our control, and these variables will influence whether our choices made today are the right ones for the long haul.

Without a doubt, one of the most common quandaries we observe with our clients is the age-old question of when to begin taking social security retirement income benefits. Is it better to take a lesser amount and begin getting benefits at an earlier age or is it better to wait and take a higher benefit amount beginning at a later age? If we had a crystal ball and could see into the future, this would be a much easier question to answer than it is without some assurance of what is around the next turn.

Perhaps, the most obvious question is "*where is the crossover between starting early at a lesser amount vs. waiting and getting a higher monthly benefit for life?*".

We hope to shed some light on that question here and help provide some guardrails and map notes as you consider this important part of your overall retirement plan.

Let's start with some basics about social security retirement income benefits.

Before we forget, however, this is a great time, if you haven't done so already, to get yourself signed up with social security, review the data that they have on file for your earnings and benefit estimates and get a snapshot of your alternatives.

www.ssa.gov

Once you have established an online account, request a Social Security Statement.

Additionally, you will find a plethora of help topics and FAQ's that will likely answer many of your initial questions including what impact there will be on your benefits if you remain working while receiving social security retirement income. Don't be afraid to poke around the website as the information available is substantive and meaningful.

Here is another great link to use for considering your choices and how they impact you and your family.

www.ssa.gov/benefits/retirement/matrix.html

Back to the basics…the age at which you start receiving Social Security benefits affects the amount you receive, with higher monthly benefits available the longer you wait to start your income:

For anyone born after 1960-

- ◊ Age 62

  You can start receiving benefits at age 62, but your monthly benefit will be 70% of your full retirement benefit.

- ◊ Age 67

  This is your full retirement age (FRA), and you'll receive your full monthly benefit.

- ◊ Age 70

  You'll receive 124% of your full monthly benefit, which is the maximum amount you can receive per year.

The Social Security Administration (SSA) will adjust benefits each year for cost of living (COLA) changes. Obviously, the longer you wait to start your income, the larger the monthly benefit amount will be that these adjustments are applied to.

Additionally, factors that affect your Social Security benefits include your work history and birth year. You can use your Social Security earnings history statement to estimate your monthly benefit at different ages.

When considering when to start receiving your Social Security retirement income benefits, you can use these factors below to hone your thinking:

◊ **Break-even crossover**: The point at which the cumulative amount you receive if you file early equals the amount you receive if you file later. This is an important step and one we said we will help you to address. As a simple guiding principle, however, if your life expectancy is before the crossover break-even age, it would seem prudent to start your benefits as early as is possible, even if you don't need the money right now. You can always save excess income for future needs and wants.

◊ **Life expectancy**: If you expect to live a long time, it might be better to wait to claim. Since break-even points discussed above may not come for a while, only if you anticipate living to or past life expectancy should you be considering delaying benefits. Of course, as always, there are complications to this decision as survivor needs are included in your consideration. There may be two of you receiving benefits while you are alive, but only one check will continue following a death-albeit the larger of the two checks, but a time when there will be a loss of income, nonetheless. So, making decisions to secure a larger primary check to the family by delaying your start date may be necessary for the surviving spouse

◊ **Annual earnings**: If you are going to remain earning income from work but want to simultaneously access benefits and it is before your Normal Retirement Age, your social security may be reduced if your annual earnings exceed a certain limit.

For 2025, if you are receiving wages while receiving social security and you are younger than your Normal Retirement Age, there will be a $1 reduction in income benefits for every $2 you earn over $23,400.

So, following the amounts noted above, as an example, if you are claiming benefits in 2025 and you earn $25,000 from work during 2025, the social security income benefits will be reduced by $800 for the year. $25,000 is $1,600 over the income limits thereby subjecting the $1,600 overage to a 1 for 2 reduction…or $800 reduction for a $1,600 overage. To pay for this reduction, you would skip your starting income benefits until the reduction is accounted for and then resume at what your monthly benefit would have been before the reduction.

The income that is considered for this potential reduction in benefits include your wages from an employer, or if self-employed, they count your net earnings from self-employment. Social Security income formulas do NOT count other government benefits, investment earnings, interest, pensions, annuities and capital gains when considering income for the income reduction calculations. Additionally, the calculations are only supposed to include earnings paid to you in a particular year, not when they were earned. So, items such as accumulated sick pay, vacation days and bonuses earned prior to when you began receiving benefits should not be included as income for determining any reductions in social security benefits.

Additionally, when calculating whether there are reductions for benefits due to work related income, your spouse's income is NOT counted in this calculation.

There are separate and special rules that apply to one-year earnings…this occurs when someone retires mid-year already having exceeded the annual earnings limit.

It is important to note here that if you choose to remain working and are receiving social security income benefits from a pre-normal retirement age and your benefits result in a reduction of monthly income due to excess earnings, once you reach normal retirement age your benefits will increase starting on your normal retirement age. If your earnings during the pre-normal retirement age period increase your overall wage records so that your highest 35-year history improves from when you started to receive benefits, you will receive the benefit of that higher calculation too once you reach normal retirement age.

Adjustments to increase benefits due to a higher average 35-year history happen automatically.

If you have taken our suggestion and visited the ssa.gov website, you will find there is a helpful booklet available titled *"How Work Affects Your Benefits"*.

Calculating your break-even point…

The process of calculating a break-even crossover time is not an exact science. There are things such as cost-of-living adjustments, the time value of money and whether you work and earn income that may cause fluctuations in these break-even calculations. You should, however, be able to arrive at a decent estimate of your break-even point.

Let's assume you are approaching the age of 62 and considering whether you should begin benefits now or wait until a later date. And let's assume your estimated monthly income at Normal Retirement Age of 67 is $2,000 per month.

Your age 62 benefit would be 70% of the $2,000 which equates to a 30% reduction due to early retirement, leaving you with a starting monthly income of $1,400. This would result in a 5-year total income benefit for the period of ages 62 to 67 of $84,000. ($1,400 per month X 60 months)

Had you waited until you were 67, you would forfeit the $84,000 but you would start at $2,000 per month for a difference of $600 more per month, or $7,200 more per year. Based upon this calculation, we can then take the $7,200 of higher benefit and divide it by the income we gave up between ages 62 and 67 and that gives us the time it takes to break even. In this case, 11.66 years. Age 67 plus 11.66 means that just before age 79 you will reach your breakeven point. In theory, each month you live past age 79, you will be ahead of the game than had you chosen to start your income at age 62.

To further determine your options, you may wish to consider delaying *past* your normal retirement date as well. With an increase to a maximum of 124% of normal retirement age amounts, your new monthly benefit at age 70 would be $2,480.

If we calculate starting at age 62 and go to age 70, that is 8 years or 96 months over which we would have received $134,400. At age 70, you'd get approximately $1,080 more per month, or $12,960 more per year. Your break-even period would be 10.37 years, leaving you a break-even age of 80.37 years old.

Beyond just the break-even calculations, however, there are other things to consider.

Your physical health, current financial needs and many other factors need to be considered when making these decisions.

Suppose you are turning 62 and are in poor health. What is the likelihood you will reach the crossover age from the calculations we showed you above? Will you live long enough to reach a point where delaying your start date makes financial sense? What about your companion in life? Will your spouse be relying on your benefits when you die? Are you still servicing debt such as a mortgage and you need the income regardless of whether it is reduced or not?

What other resources do you have to work with? Are there retirement accounts such as IRA and 401(k) that are available for income? Do you *want* to keep working and if so, how much can you earn either full or part-time working while receiving benefits from social security?

Social Security and Income Taxes

At the time we are publishing this book, the current administration in Washington DC is actively seeking new tax code that would eliminate income taxes on social security benefits completely. Whether that comes to fruition or not remains to be seen and if so, everyone that is currently paying taxes on their social security benefits will be getting a welcome pay raise.

The maximum social security benefit in 2024 for someone retiring at normal retirement age is just under $46,000 per year. The maximum that can be considered for income taxes is 85%, or in this example, about $39,000.

While social security is not intended to be someone's sole source of retirement income, it remains a significant component of an overall retirement plan for our clients and managing and understanding taxes is important to achieving tax efficiency in your overall retirement planning strategy.

Income taxation on Social Security benefits is based on what the Social Security Administration (SSA) refers to as your "combined" income. That consists of your adjusted gross income, plus any nontaxable interest you earn (and certain other items) and half of your Social Security income. The thresholds for when your benefits will be taxable vary based on your filing status as shown in the chart below.

Exhibit 15.

Social Security federal income tax

Married filing jointly	
Your combined annual income	How much of your Social Security benefit is taxable
$32,000 or less	None
Between $32,000 and $44,000	Up to 50%
More than $44,000	Up to 85%
Individual	

Your combined annual income	How much of your Social Security benefit is taxable
$25,000 or less	None
Between $25,000 and $34,000	Up to 50%
More than $34,000	Up to 85%

Let's look at some factors for you to consider to minimizing taxes and maximize usable income.

The long view

You can't just look at today when strategizing for income taxes. Consider a longer view in your planning and whether there are ways to organize how you receive income. For example, if you have situations where you are coming into large lump sums of money, perhaps structuring that income to be paid in installments over time is a better way to receive that income, spreading the income receipt over time instead of taking receipt of those funds all at once and moving yourself into a much higher tax bracket.

Timing...

How and from where you take your income will impact income taxes. Assuming you have resources that are treated differently for income tax purposes, such as IRA and ROTH IRA accounts. You should plan the timing of the income from these sources to best minimize income taxes which includes choosing the timing for income sources that might impact social security income calculations.

Special Note: Roth IRA withdrawals are not counted as income and won't increase taxes on your Social Security benefits.

Other Financial Resources...

Assets that can be converted into income streams over time may help you position yourself to smooth out larger swings in income and help you plan and manage your income tax situation in a better way. Couple this consideration with the need or desire to continue working and refresh yourself on the impact of earning wages while receiving benefits from social security. And don't forget, as mentioned earlier, your spouses' wages do not impact your limits for income in determining if there will be any social security income reductions due to earned wages while receiving benefits. So, your spouse can continue to work while one of you may opt for starting benefits at an age prior to your normal retirement age.

To clarify this point, income earned by a spouse does NOT count against you in determining if you reach income limits that would reduce benefits if you are working and claiming benefits prior to your normal retirement age, but the spouses income IS counted when filing a joint tax return in determining if any or a portion of your social security benefit is taxable or not.

These considerations are all very good discussion points for you to have with us as your financial sherpa.

What did we learn or confirm here?

1. Social Security is not designed to provide 100% of your retirement income needs. Ideally you have other resources in addition to Social Security and the extent to which you have other resources will dictate the role Social Security Income will play in your overall plans

2. You do not have to begin receiving benefits at age 70 but there is no financial incentive to delay past age 70.

3. You should take advantage of the information provided by visiting www.ssa.gov as there is an abundance of value in this online portal.

4. There is no single answer to the question of the best age to start receiving Social Security benefits or to the question of whether you should continue working if you elect to claim benefits prior to age 67. Everyone's situation is a little bit different and considering and weighing your own circumstances will provide you with the best answer to this query. We are here to help you with this important consideration.

5. A break-even analysis to help you determine when you should elect commencing benefits is a good tool to use in helping you make an informed decision about your benefit potential.

CHAPTER TEN

WHICH ONE WHEN?

There are a plethora of retirement plans out there and just as you have choices for the types of gear to wear and bring along for your journey to and through the summit, you also have choices for the manufacturers of that gear. Sometimes you don't have a choice as to what you wear while other folks may have total freedom as to who's gear they choose to buy and how they choose to use that gear.

So, too, is the world of retirement plans. In some cases you will be choosing the types of plans you need to best save for retirement, and those that will serve you best in distributing income during retirement and for others, those plans will be chosen for you as employer sponsored plans. It is very typical for folks to have a combination of these plans during their working and retired lives.

The following is a partial list of various retirement plans available today.

Individual Retirement Arrangements (IRAs)
ROTH IRAs

401(k) plans
SIMPLE 401(k) plans
403(b) plans, sometimes referred to as TSA plans

SIMPLE IRA plans (Savings Incentive Match Plans for Employees)
SEP plans (Simplified Employee Pension)
SARSEP plans (Salary Reduction Simplified Employee Pension)
Payroll deduction IRAs
Profit-sharing plans
Defined benefit plans
Money purchase plans
Employee stock ownership plans (ESOPs)
401(a) plans

457 plans

In our business, most of our clients come to us after having been a participant in an employer sponsored defined contribution plan such as a 401(k) and they are looking for options as to how to move that money out of their work related retirement plan and into their own plan such as an IRA where they can now choose from far more options as to the underlying investments of those funds as well as applying funds to other types of programs that can best serve their income planning needs.

It is beyond the scope of this book to get into the details of every one of these types of retirement plans. Suffice it to say, though, that there are different rules for many of these plans and your options may or may not be as clear as one might think they should be.

It is good to point out here that the types of accounts listed above fall into what we refer to as rules-based money. There are several rules and regulations that govern each of the types of plans noted. Understanding the rules for your plan(s) is crucial to understanding how best to coordinate your income planning across all your financial resources and should consider the income tax treatment of money that will be available for income planning in the years ahead.

One easy way to keep track of taxation on these types of programs is simply to remember, if you get to deduct income at the time you make contributions to a plan, then when you access these money at a later date, the contributions you made as well as any earnings on your money will be fully taxable to you as they are paid to you. If you do not deduct contributions, in other words your contributions to a plan are made with after-tax dollars, then you avoid taxation later when you access the funds. This is a very general statement and does not apply in all situations, but it is a good rule of thumb to understand going into the planning process. In the basic example above, think of tax-deductible contributions to an IRA versus after-tax contributions to a ROTH. While there are some rules for ROTH plans that can impact the tax-free status of distributions, generally the rules apply as stated; IRA distribution will be 100% taxable income to you and ROTH distributions will be 100% tax-free to you.

In times from the past, it was a common planning predicate that deferring taxes today and delaying payment on the taxes until a later time (typically retirement) was always the prudent thing to do. That financial equation is not as simple as it seems and the lure to defer current taxation is strong. It happens every day by default without much contemplation of the results overall. While we agree that avoiding taxes is an important goal in planning for net income, we don't necessarily agree that tax avoidance should always be at the front end of the equation.

The predicate is based on the idea or notion that you will always be in a lower tax bracket at retirement than you are today while working and receiving employment income. This predicate is flawed, however, and is one of the reasons ROTH plans have come into existence as well as many other options for savings that result in similar tax treatment as a ROTH, in other words, producing non-taxable income to you from sources that would otherwise generate taxable income to you to the extent there is gain on your money from your investment returns.

There is no guarantee you will be in a lower tax bracket at the time you receive retirement income than you were when you deducted contributions to a plan. Other rules will be applicable too at retirement and tax planning needs to consider all sides of the equation. In the prior chapter we discussed taxation of social security benefits, as an example. As of today, receiving fully taxable income from an IRA or a 401(k) plan may subject your social security income to taxation that might not otherwise occur if receiving non-taxable income. So, in this case we avoided some tax at the front end only to incur additional taxes later due to IRS regulations.

Also, while we know there is much consideration in Washington, DC right now about tax code and income tax rates and rate thresholds changing in favor of lower income taxes, both the magnitude of the financial woes we have in this country including over 36 *trillion* dollars in debt, legislators who can't seem to adhere to a balanced budget and a plethora of wrongs that need to be put right in this country that will cost billions in taxpayer dollars, it is hard to assume we will see much reprieve in the foreseeable future. In fact, we may find ourselves in higher brackets at retirement than we had when working.

Additionally, and something we discuss often with our clients is that when you have buckets of money that have rules attached to them, such as IRA "Required Minimum Distributions", you must be careful with the timing of distributions. Kicking the can down the road with rules-based money can be a trap for income taxes that will not serve you well. Sometimes you are better off smoothing out the income over time and maintaining a lower bracket than pushing everything taxable out to a later date and find yourself having to take much larger distributions than you need due to required distribution rules. And, by pushing all the fully-taxable money out as far as you can, you also subject your non-spouse beneficiaries to rules that force full distribution of that money within 10 years of your death, potentially pushing the money into tax brackets far higher than they needed to be.

This is why we look at options at times such as converting IRA money to ROTH money in increments, paying tax today on these incremental transactions and avoiding any future income tax on that money as well as any future earnings. Whether ROTH conversions are something for you depends upon several factors, but the point is that income tax planning should include a look at the impact of taxes on net spendable income and ideally be using an organized distribution plan in a way that results in the most efficient way to receive your retirement income.

If you were a farmer, would you rather pay taxes on the seed you plant, or the harvest you ultimately reap from the fields? We would contend there are many, many cases where the biggest benefit will come from paying tax today on the seed, a much smaller number, and never pay tax on the harvest, ever.

In moving money from an employer sponsored plan to your own individual plan or plans, such as an IRA, the transaction is typically done as a *direct rollover* from the work plan to your own individual plan without incurring any tax liability on the transfer. The rules of your employer plan will govern how, when and *if* you can roll over funds to your own plan. Some folks can move their employer sponsored plan monies while they are still employed, others may have to wait until they sever their work relationship. Sometimes money contributed by the employee is treated differently than money that is in your account as the result of an employer's contribution to your plan. The point is, as seems to be the case with so many things we do in our business, very little is the same from one situation to the next. It is important to understand your plan and be aware of how, when and if you can rollover your funds and know what limitations might apply in your situation.

Let's look at a traditional IRA as well as some recent changes to IRA and ROTH IRAs. Even though we typically are dealing with *rollover* IRAs and planning for how to distribute funds over time at retirement, some of the information noted below refers to the context of an IRA or ROTH IRA as if you are continuing to contribute money.

A traditional IRA is a way to save for retirement that gives you tax advantages.

◊ Contributions you make to a traditional IRA may be fully or partially deductible, depending on your filing status and income, and

◊ Generally, amounts in your traditional IRA (including earnings and gains) are not taxed until you take a distribution (withdrawal) from your IRA.

Some recent changes…What's New for 2024

◊ IRA contribution limit increased for 2024. Beginning in 2024, the IRA contribution limit is increased to $7,000 ($8,000 for individuals age 50 or older) from $6,500 ($7,500 for individuals age 50 or older).

◊ Distributions to victims of domestic abuse. Beginning with distributions made after December 31, 2023, a distribution to a domestic abuse victim is not subject to the 10% additional tax on early distributions if the distribution meets certain requirements.

◊ Distributions for emergency personal expenses. Beginning with distributions made after December 31, 2023, Department of the Treasury Internal Revenue Service the exception to the 10% additional tax for early distributions is expanded to include distributions for certain emergency personal expenses.

◊ Qualified tuition program rollover to a Roth IRA. Beginning with distributions made after December 31, 2023, a beneficiary of a section 529 qualified tuition program is permitted to roll over a distribution from a section 529 account into a Roth IRA for the beneficiary if certain requirements are met.

◊ Modified AGI limit for traditional IRA contributions. For 2024, if you are covered by a retirement plan at work, your deduction for contributions to a traditional IRA is reduced (phased out) if your modified AGI is:

- More than $123,000 but less than $143,000 for a married couple filing a joint return or a qualifying surviving spouse,

- More than $77,000 but less than $87,000 for a single individual or head of household, or
- Less than $10,000 for a married individual filing a separate return.

◊ Modified AGI limit for certain married individuals.

- If you are married and your spouse is covered by a retirement plan at work and you aren't, and you live with your spouse or file a joint return, your deduction is phased out if your modified AGI is more than $230,000 (up from $218,000 for 2023) but less than $240,000 (up from $228,000 for 2023). If your modified AGI is $240,000 or more, you can't take a deduction for contributions to a traditional IRA.

◊ Modified AGI limit for Roth IRA contributions.

- For 2024, your Roth IRA contribution limit is reduced (phased out) in the following situations.
    - Your filing status is married filing jointly or qualifying surviving spouse and your modified AGI is at least $230,000. You can't make a Roth IRA contribution if your modified AGI is $240,000 or more.
    - Your filing status is single, head of household, or married filing separately and you didn't live with your spouse at any time in 2024 and your modified AGI is at least $146,000. You can't make a Roth IRA contribution if your modified AGI is $161,000 or more.

- Your filing status is married filing separately, you lived with your spouse at any time during the year, and your modified AGI is more than zero. You can't make a Roth IRA contribution if your modified AGI is $10,000 or more.

More current changes… What's New for 2025 IRA and ROTH IRA

IRA contribution limit for 2025

◊ For 2025, the IRA contribution limit remains $7,000 ($8,000 for individuals age 50 or older).

◊ Modified AGI limit for traditional IRA contributions increased.

- For 2025, if you are covered by a retirement plan at work, your deduction for contributions to a traditional IRA is reduced (phased out) if your modified AGI is:
    - More than $126,000 but less than $146,000 for a married couple filing a joint return or a qualifying surviving spouse,
    - More than $79,000 but less than $89,000 for a single individual or head of household, or
    - Less than $10,000 for a married individual filing a separate return.

◊ Modified AGI limit for certain married individuals increased.

- If you are married and your spouse is covered by a retirement plan at work and you aren't, and you live with your spouse or file a joint return, your deduction is phased out if your modified AGI is more than $236,000 (up from $230,000 for 2024) but less than $246,000 (up from $240,000 for 2024).

- If your modified AGI is $246,000 or more, you can't take a deduction for contributions to a traditional IRA.

◊ Modified AGI limit for Roth IRA contributions increased.

◊ For 2025, your Roth IRA contribution limit is reduced (phased out) in the following situations.

◊ Your filing status is married filing jointly or qualifying surviving spouse and your modified AGI is at least $236,000. You can't make a Roth IRA contribution if your modified AGI is $246,000 or more.

  - Your filing status is single, head of household, or married filing separately and you didn't live with your spouse at any time in 2025 and your modified AGI is at east $150,000.

◊ You can't make a Roth IRA contribution if your modified AGI is $165,000 or more.

  - Your filing status is married filing separately, you lived with your spouse at any time during the year, and your modified AGI is more than zero.
  - You can't make a Roth IRA contribution if your modified AGI is $10,000 or more.

Reminders

◊ Increase in required minimum distribution age.

    - Individuals who reach age 72 after December 31, 2022, may delay receiving their required minimum distributions (RMDs) until April 1 of the year following the year in which they turn age 73.

◊ Qualified disaster tax relief.

    - The special rules that provide for tax-favored withdrawals and repayments from certain qualified plans for taxpayers who suffered an economic loss as a result of a qualified disaster were made permanent by the SECURE 2.0 Act of 2022. A qualified disaster is a major disaster that occurred on or after January 26, 2021, and was declared by the President after December 27, 2020, under section 401 of the Robert T. Stafford Disaster Relief and Emergency Act.

◊ Beginning on December 29, 2022, the 10% additional tax on early distributions will not apply to a corrective IRA distribution, which consists of an excess contribution (a contribution greater than the IRA contribution limit) and any earnings allocable to the excess contribution, as long as the corrective distribution is made on or before the due date (including extensions) of the income tax return.

◊ Divorce or separation instruments after 2018.

    - Amounts paid as alimony or separate maintenance payments under a divorce or separation instrument executed after 2018 won't be deductible by the payer. Such amounts also won't be includible in the income of the recipient. The same is true of alimony paid under a divorce or separation instrument executed before 2019 and modified after 2018, if the modification expressly states that the alimony isn't deductible to the payer or includible in the income of the recipient.

◊ IRA interest.

- Although interest earned from your IRA is generally not taxed in the year earned, it isn't tax-exempt interest. Tax on your traditional IRA is generally deferred until you take a distribution. Don't report this interest on your return as tax-exempt interest. For more information on tax-exempt interest, see the instructions for your tax return.

What are some tax advantages of an IRA?

Two tax advantages of an IRA are that:

◊ Contributions you make to an IRA may be fully or partially deductible, depending on which type of IRA you have and on your circumstances; and

◊ Generally, amounts in your IRA (including earnings and gains) aren't taxed until distributed.

Traditional IRAs

A traditional IRA is any IRA that isn't a Roth IRA or a SIMPLE IRA.

Who Can Open a Traditional IRA?

You can open and make contributions to a traditional IRA if you (or, if you file a joint return, your spouse) receive taxable compensation during the year. You can have a traditional IRA whether or not you are covered by any other retirement plan. However, you may not be able to deduct all of your contributions if you or your spouse is covered by an employer retirement plan.

If both you and your spouse have compensation, each of you can open an IRA. You can't both participate in the same IRA. If you file a joint return, only one of you needs to have compensation.

What Is Compensation?

Generally, compensation is what you earn from working. Compensation includes wages, salaries, tips, professional fees, bonuses, and other amounts you receive for providing personal services are compensation. If you are self-employed (a sole proprietor or a partner), compensation is the net earnings from your trade or business (provided your personal services are a material income-producing factor) reduced by the total of:

◊ The deduction for contributions made on your behalf to retirement plans, and

◊ The deduction allowed for the deductible part of your self-employment taxes.

Compensation includes earnings from self-employment even if they aren't subject to self-employment tax because of your religious beliefs.

Self-employment loss. If you have a net loss from self-employment, don't subtract the loss from your salaries or wages when figuring out your total compensation.

Alimony and separate maintenance. For IRA purposes, compensation includes any taxable alimony and separate maintenance payments you receive under a decree of divorce or separate maintenance but only with respect to divorce or separation instruments executed on or before December 31, 2018, that have not been modified to exclude such amounts.

Nontaxable combat pay. If you were a member of the U.S. Armed Forces, compensation includes any nontaxable combat pay you received. This amount should be reported in box 12 of your 2024 Form W-2 with code Q.

Graduate or postdoctoral study. A scholarship or fellowship is generally taxable compensation only if it is in box 1 of your Form W-2. However, for tax years beginning after 2019, certain non-tuition fellowship and stipend payments not reported to you on Form W-2 are treated as taxable compensation for IRA purposes. These amounts include taxable non-tuition fellowship and stipend payments made to aid you in the pursuit of graduate or postdoctoral study and included in your gross income.

What *Isn't* Compensation?

Compensation *doesn't* include any of the following items.

- ◊ Earnings and profits from property, such as rental income, interest income, and dividend income.
- ◊ Pension or annuity income.
- ◊ Deferred compensation received (compensation payments postponed from a past year).
- ◊ Income from a partnership for which you don't provide services that are a material income-producing factor.
- ◊ Conservation Reserve Program (CRP) payments reported on Schedule SE (Form 1040), line 1b.
- ◊ Any amounts (other than combat pay) you exclude from income, such as foreign earned income and housing costs.

When Can a Traditional IRA Be Opened?

You can open a traditional IRA at any time. However, the time for making contributions for any year is limited.

You can open different kinds of IRAs with a variety of organizations. You can open an IRA at a bank or other financial institution or with a mutual fund or life insurance company. You can also open an IRA through your stockbroker. Any IRA must meet Internal Revenue Code requirements.

An individual retirement account is a trust or custodial account set up in the United States for the exclusive benefit of you or your beneficiaries. The account is created by a written document. The document must show that the account meets all of the following requirements.

◊ The trustee or custodian must be a bank, a federally insured credit union, a savings and loan association, or an entity approved by the IRS to act as trustee or custodian.

◊ The trustee or custodian generally can't accept contributions of more than the deductible amount for the year. However, rollover contributions and employer contributions to a SEP can be more than this amount.

◊ Contributions, except for rollover contributions, must be in cash.

◊ You must have a nonforfeitable right to the amount at all times.

◊ Money in your account can't be used to buy a life insurance policy.

◊ Assets in your account can't be combined with other property, except in a common trust fund or common investment fund.

◊ You must start receiving distributions by April 1 of the year following the year in which you reach the age of 73. See Pub. 590-B for more information about RMDs and other distribution rules.

Individual Retirement Annuity

You can open an individual retirement annuity by purchasing an annuity contract or an endowment contract from a life insurance company. An individual retirement annuity must be issued in your name as the owner, and either you or your beneficiaries who survive you are the only ones who can receive the benefits or payments.

An individual retirement annuity must meet all the following requirements.

◊ Your entire interest in the contract must be nonforfeitable.

◊ The contract must provide that you can't transfer any portion of it to any person other than the issuer.

◊ There must be flexible premiums so that if your compensation changes, your payment can also change. This provision applies to contracts issued after November 6, 1978.

◊ The contract must provide that contributions can't be more than the deductible amount for an IRA for the year, and that you must use any refunded premiums to pay for future premiums or to buy more benefits before the end of the calendar year after the year in which you receive the refund.

◊ Distributions must begin by April 1 of the year following the year in which you reach the age of 73. See Pub. 590-B for more information about RMDs and other distribution rules.

When Must You Withdraw Assets? (Required Minimum Distributions)

You can't keep funds in a traditional IRA (including SEP and SIMPLE IRAs) indefinitely. Eventually, they must be distributed. If there are no distributions, or if the distributions aren't large enough, you may have to pay an excise tax on the amount not distributed as required. See Excess Accumulations (Insufficient Distributions), later, under What Acts Result in Penalties or Additional Taxes. The requirements for distributing IRA funds differ, depending on whether you are the IRA owner or the beneficiary of a decedent's IRA.

Required minimum distribution (RMD).

The amount that must be distributed each year is referred to as the required minimum distribution. Note. A qualified charitable distribution will count towards your required minimum distribution.

◊ IRA Owners Required beginning date.

If you are the owner of a traditional IRA, you must generally start receiving distributions from your IRA by April 1 of the year following the year in which you reach age 72 (or age 73). April 1 of the year following the year in which you reach age 72 (or age 73, as applicable) is referred to as the "required beginning date." Note. Individuals who reach age 72 in tax years beginning after December 31, 2022, may delay receiving their required minimum distributions until April 1 of the year following the year in which they reach age 73.

Your required beginning date. The date you must begin receiving RMDs is determined by the date you reach age 72.

See the following to determine your applicable required beginning date.

Age 72 after December 31, 2022. If you reach age 72 after December 31, 2022, you must begin receiving required minimum distributions by April 1 of the year following the year you reach the age 73.

Age 72 in tax years 2020, 2021, or 2022. If you were born after June 30, 1949, you must begin receiving required minimum distributions by April 1 of the year following the year you reach age 72.

Age 70 ½ for tax years 2019 or earlier. If you were born before July 1, 1949, you were required to begin receiving required minimum distributions by April 1 of the year following the year you reach age 70 ½.

Distributions by the required beginning date.

You must receive at least a minimum amount for each year starting on your required beginning date. If an IRA owner dies after reaching age 72 (or age 73), but before their required beginning date, no minimum distribution is required for that year because death occurred before the required beginning date. Even if you begin receiving distributions before you reach age 72 (or age 73, if applicable), you must begin calculating and receiving RMDs by your required beginning date.

More than minimum received. If, in any year, you receive more than the required minimum distribution for that year, you won't receive credit for the additional amount when determining the required minimum distributions for future years. This doesn't mean that you don't reduce your IRA account balance. It means that if you receive more than your required minimum distribution in 1 year, you can't treat the excess (the amount that is more than the required minimum distribution) as part of your required minimum distribution for any later year. However, any amount distributed in the year you become age 72 (or age 73) will be credited toward the amount that must be distributed by April 1 of the following year.

Distributions after the required beginning date.

The required minimum distribution for any year after the year you reach the age of 72 (or age 73) must be made by December 31 of that later year.

Distributions from individual retirement accounts. If you are the owner of a traditional IRA that is an individual retirement account, you or your trustee must figure the required minimum distribution for each year.

Distributions from individual retirement annuities. If your traditional IRA is an individual retirement annuity, special rules apply to figuring the required minimum distribution.

◊ Change in marital status.

For the purposes of figuring your required minimum distribution, your marital status is determined as of January 1 of each year. If your spouse is a beneficiary of your IRA on January 1, they will remain a beneficiary for the entire year even if you get divorced or your spouse dies during the year. For purposes of determining your distribution period, a change in beneficiary is effective in the year following the year of death or divorce.

◊ Change of beneficiary.

If your spouse is the sole beneficiary of your IRA, and they die before you, your spouse won't fail to be your sole beneficiary for the year they died solely because someone other than your spouse is named a beneficiary for the rest of that year. However, if you get divorced during the year and change the beneficiary designation on the IRA during that same year, your former spouse won't be treated as the sole beneficiary for that year.

Figuring the Owner's Required Minimum Distribution

Figure your required minimum distribution for each year by dividing the IRA account balance (defined next) as of the close of business on December 31 of the preceding year by the applicable distribution period or life expectancy.

IRA account balance. The IRA account balance is the amount in the IRA at the end of the year preceding the year for which the required minimum distribution is being figured.

Contributions. Contributions increase the account balance in the year they are made. If a contribution for last year isn't made until after December 31 of last year, it increases the account balance for this year, but not for last year.

Disregard contributions made after December 31 of last year in determining your required minimum distribution for this year.

Outstanding rollovers. The IRA account balance is adjusted by outstanding rollovers that aren't in any account at the end of the preceding year. For a rollover from a qualified plan or another IRA that wasn't in any account at the end of the preceding year, increase the account balance of the receiving IRA by the rollover amount valued as of the date of receipt.

No recharacterizations of conversions made in 2018 or later. A conversion of a traditional IRA to a Roth IRA, and a rollover from any other eligible retirement plan to a Roth IRA, made in tax years beginning after December 31, 2017, cannot be recharacterized as having been made to a traditional IRA.

Distributions. Distributions reduce the account balance in the year they are made. A distribution for last year made after December 31 of last year reduces the account balance for this year, but not for last year.

Disregard distributions made after December 31 of last year in determining your required minimum distribution for this year.

Distribution period.

This is the number by which you divide your account balance as of December 31 of last year to calculate your required minimum distribution.

Distributions during your lifetime.

Required minimum distributions during your lifetime are based on a distribution period that is generally determined using Table III (Uniform Lifetime). Exceptions apply if your spouse is more than 10 years younger than you. To figure the required minimum distribution for 2024, divide your account balance at the end of 2023 by the distribution period from the table.

Distributions in the year of the owner's death.

The required minimum distribution for the year of the owner's death depends on whether the owner died before the required beginning date, defined earlier. If the owner died before the required beginning date, there is no required minimum distribution in the year of the owner's death.

If the owner died on or after the required beginning date, the IRA beneficiaries are responsible for figuring and distributing the owner's required minimum distribution in the year of death. The owner's required minimum distribution for the year of death is generally based on Table III (Uniform Lifetime). However, if the sole beneficiary of the IRA is the owner's spouse who is more than 10 years younger than the owner, use the life expectancy from Table II (Joint Life and Last Survivor Expectancy). Note. You figure the required minimum distribution for the year in which an IRA owner dies as if the owner lived for the entire year.

IRA Beneficiaries

The rules for determining the required minimum distributions for beneficiaries depend on whether:

◊ • The beneficiary is the surviving spouse.

◊ • The beneficiary is an eligible designated beneficiary (defined later) other than the surviving spouse.

◊ • The beneficiary is an individual (other than an eligible designated beneficiary).

◊ • The beneficiary isn't an individual (for example, the beneficiary is the owner's estate). (But see Trust as beneficiary, later, for a discussion about treating trust beneficiaries as designated beneficiaries.)

◊ • The IRA owner died before the required beginning date or died on or after the required beginning date.

Penalties or Additional Taxes?

The tax advantages of using traditional IRAs for retirement savings can be offset by additional taxes and penalties if you don't follow the rules. There are additions to the regular tax for using your IRA funds in prohibited transactions. There are also additional taxes for the following activities.

◊ • Investing in collectibles.

◊ • Having unrelated business income.

◊ • Taking early distributions.

◊ • Allowing excess amounts to accumulate (failing to take required distributions).

◊ • Making excess contributions. There are penalties for overstating the amount of nondeductible contributions and for failure to file Form 8606, if required.

Prohibited Transactions Generally

A prohibited transaction is any improper use of your traditional IRA account or annuity by you, your beneficiary, or any disqualified person. Disqualified persons include your fiduciary and members of your family (spouse, ancestor, lineal descendant, and any spouse of a lineal descendant). The following are some examples of prohibited transactions with a traditional IRA.

- ◊ Borrowing money from it.
- ◊ Selling property to it.
- ◊ Using it as security for a loan.
- ◊ Buying property for personal use (present or future) with IRA funds. If your IRA invested in non-publicly traded assets or assets that you directly control, the risk of engaging in a prohibited transaction in connection with your IRA may be increased.

Fiduciary.

A fiduciary includes anyone who does any of the following.

- ◊ • Exercises any discretionary authority or discretionary control in managing your IRA or exercises any authority or control in managing or disposing of its assets.
- ◊ • Provides investment advice to your IRA for a fee or has any authority or responsibility to do so.
- ◊ • Has any discretionary authority or discretionary responsibility in administering your IRA.

Effect on an IRA account.

Generally, if you or your beneficiary engages in a prohibited transaction in connection with your traditional IRA account at any time during the year, the account stops being an IRA as of the first day of that year. However, if you own more than one IRA, each IRA is treated as a separate account, and loss of IRA status only affects that IRA that participated in that prohibited transaction.

Effect on you or your beneficiary.

If your account stops being an IRA because you or your beneficiary engaged in a prohibited transaction, the account is treated as distributing all its assets to you at their fair market values on the first day of the year. If the total of those values is more than your basis in the IRA, you will have a taxable gain that is includible in your income. The distribution may be subject to additional taxes or penalties.

Borrowing on an annuity contract.

If you borrow money against your traditional IRA annuity contract, you must include in your gross income the fair market value of the annuity contract as of the first day of your tax year. You may have to pay the 10% additional tax on early distributions, discussed later.

Pledging an account as security.

If you use a part of your traditional IRA account as security for a loan, that part is treated as a distribution and is included in your gross income. You may have to pay the 10% penalty.

Taxes on prohibited transactions.

If someone other than the owner or beneficiary of a traditional IRA engages in a prohibited transaction, that person may be liable for certain taxes. In general, there is a 15% tax on the prohibited transaction and a 100% additional tax if the transaction isn't corrected. Loss of IRA status. If the traditional IRA ceases to be an IRA because of a prohibited transaction by you or your beneficiary, neither you nor your beneficiary is liable for these excise taxes. However, you or your beneficiary may have to pay other taxes.

Exempt Transactions

The Department of Labor has authority to grant administrative exemptions from the prohibited transaction provisions of ERISA and the Code for a class of transactions or for individual transactions. To grant an administrative exemption, the Department must make the following three determinations. 1. The exemption must be administratively feasible. 2. In the interest of the plan and its participants and beneficiaries. 3. Protective of the rights of plan participants and beneficiaries.

The following two types of transactions aren't prohibited transactions if they meet the requirements that follow.

◊ Payments of cash, property, or other consideration by the sponsor of your traditional IRA to you (or members of your family).

◊ Your receipt of services at reduced or no cost from the bank where your traditional IRA is established or maintained. Payments of cash, property, or other consideration. Even if a sponsor makes payments to you or your family, there is no prohibited transaction if all three of the following requirements are met. 1. The payments are for establishing a traditional IRA or for making additional contributions to it. 2. The IRA is established solely to benefit you, your spouse, and your or your spouse's beneficiaries. 3. During the year, the total fair market value of the payments you receive isn't more than: a. $10 for IRA deposits of less than $5,000, or b. $20 for IRA deposits of $5,000 or more. If the consideration is group-term life insurance, requirements (1) and (3) don't apply if no more than $5,000 of the face value of the insurance is based on a dollar-for-dollar basis on the assets in your IRA. Services received at reduced or no cost.

Even if a sponsor provides services at reduced or no cost, there is no prohibited transaction if all the following requirements are met.

◊ The traditional IRA qualifying you to receive the services is established and maintained for the benefit of you, your spouse, and your or your spouse's beneficiaries. • The bank itself can legally offer the services.

◊ The services are provided in the ordinary course of business by the bank (or a bank affiliate) to customers who qualify for but don't maintain an IRA (or a Keogh plan).

◊ The determination, for a traditional IRA, of who qualifies for these services is based on an IRA (or a Keogh plan) deposit balance equal to the lowest qualifying balance for any other type of account.

◊ The rate of return on a traditional IRA investment that qualifies isn't less than the return on an identical investment that could have been made at the same time at the same branch of the bank by a customer who isn't eligible for (or doesn't receive) these services.

Investment in Collectibles

If your traditional IRA invests in collectibles, the amount invested is considered distributed to you in the year invested. You may have to pay the 10% additional tax on early distributions. Any amounts that were considered to be distributed when the investment in the collectible was made, and which were included in your income at that time, aren't included in your income when the collectible is actually distributed from your IRA.

Collectibles. These include:

- ◊ Artworks
- ◊ Rugs
- ◊ Antiques
- ◊ Metals
- ◊ Gems
- ◊ Stamps
- ◊ Coins

Exception. Your IRA can invest in one, one-half, one-quarter, or one-tenth ounce U.S. gold coins, or one-ounce silver coins minted by the Treasury Department. It can also invest in certain platinum coins and certain gold, silver, palladium, and platinum bullion. The coins must be in the possession of the custodian or trustee of the IRA. If the owner or the beneficiary of the IRA takes possession of the coins, the coins will be treated as distributed.

Unrelated Business Income

An IRA is subject to tax on unrelated business income if it carries on an unrelated trade or business. An unrelated trade or business means any trade or business regularly carried on by the IRA or by a partnership of which it is a member, and not substantially related to the IRA's exempt purpose or function. If the IRA has $1,000 or more of unrelated trade or business gross income, the IRA must file a Form 990-T, Exempt Organization Business Income Tax Return. An IRA trustee is permitted to file Form 990-T on behalf of the IRA. In the case of an IRA that operates on a calendar year, the Form 990-T must be filed by April 15 following the close of the calendar year. In the case of an IRA that operates on a fiscal year, the Form 990-T must be filed by the 15th day of the 4th month following the close of the fiscal year.

Early Distributions

You must include early distributions of taxable amounts from your traditional IRA in your gross income. Early distributions are also subject to an additional 10% tax.

Early distributions are generally amounts distributed from your traditional IRA account or annuity before you are age 59 1/2, or amounts you receive when you cash in retirement bonds before you are age 591/2.

Age 59 1/2 Rule- Generally, if you are under age 591/2, you must pay a 10% additional tax on the distribution of any assets (money or other property) from your traditional IRA. Distributions before you are age 59 1/2 are called "early distributions." The 10% additional tax applies to the part of the distribution that you have to include in gross income. It is in addition to any regular income tax on that amount.

Exceptions There are several exceptions to the age 591/2 rule. Even if you receive a distribution before you are age 591/2, you may not have to pay the 10% additional tax if you are in one of the following situations.

- ◊ You have unreimbursed medical expenses that are more than 7.5% of your AGI.
- ◊ The distribution is for the cost of your medical insurance due to a period of unemployment.

◊ • You are totally and permanently disabled.

◊ • You have been certified as having a terminal illness.

◊ You are the beneficiary of a deceased IRA owner.

◊ You are receiving distributions in the form of a series of substantially equal periodic payments.

◊ The distribution is for your qualified higher education expenses.

◊ You use the distributions to buy, build, or rebuild a first home.

◊ The distribution is due to an IRS levy of the IRA or retirement plan.

◊ The distribution is a qualified reservist distribution.

◊ The distribution is a qualified birth or adoption distribution.

◊ The distribution is a qualified disaster distribution or qualified disaster recovery distribution.

◊ The distribution is a corrective distribution.

What did we learn or confirm here?

1. There are several retirement plan types and each has its own rules and regulations that are important for us to understand

2. We will likely have a combination of employer sponsored plan funds as well as individual retirement plan accounts

3. Understanding taxation on various types of accounts helps determine how to organize and distribute retirement funds in the most tax efficient way

4. Saving money on a pre-tax basis is not always the most efficient way to save for retirement

5. There are ways to re-characterize pre-tax monies before retirement that may help in considering tax planning strategies

CHAPTER ELEVEN

INHERITED RETIREMENT PLANS

Imagine you have approached and turned the corner on the summit, you've evaluated your supplies and considered the hazards ahead and made your plans for your descent. You start your way down and someone comes to greet you with an extra supply of oxygen, some additional rations, including an extra water supply. The relief that can be provided by these extras sounds great and allows you to perhaps re-evaluate your options ahead. During your excitement for the new supplies, you barely overhear the rules the guide gave you for utilizing the new supplies...you have 24 hours to eat the rations, drink the extra water and deplete the oxygen you thought you had for the remainder of the journey.

Poof...the excitement you had for the relief supplies now turns to anxiety as you try to figure out how you can best utilize these supplies without wasting them simply to use them up in time to meet the rules that came with them. It is now going to take some time and effort to coordinate how these fit into your original plan and how best not to waste what you have available to you. You're dismayed as you just saw another climber receive similar supply enhancements yet theirs didn't come with the same rules as you were given. That just doesn't seem right.

So, it is what it is and you re-plan your descent with these new supplies, you've figured out how to integrate the rules for using the supplies and you continue upon your descent. You get to your next trail marker having used up some of your fresh supplies and the signpost says the rules have changed and you no longer need to use these supplies within 24 hours. You can manage the supply now for up to 96 hours -but if you haven't used them all by time 96 hours comes along, you must dispose of the rest of the supplies depleting them altogether at that time.

We know the circumstance above seems hard to imagine, but the rules surrounding Inherited Retirement Plan monies has literally been that crazy for the last few years. Nobody has known what to do, the rules have changed multiple times and the recipients of inherited funds have been left confused and uneasy about the rules they must follow to stay out of hot water with the IRS in terms of how they are receiving inherited retirement plan funds.

As of the writing of this book, there has been *some* clarity brought to the table by the IRS so we are going to do our best to try and give you at least the basics on inherited retirement plans. This is probably not a road you should travel alone. We have seen several people over the last couple of years who have been given poor information and who have established distribution plans that are not as favorable as they could have been had they received better guidance when the funds were received. If you anticipate inheriting retirement plan monies from someone, this includes 401(k) assets, IRA's etc. then you should seek guidance from your financial sherpa to get the best view of your options and coordinate that as best you can into your larger plan for retirement.

As we have discussed multiple times, efficient income planning requires attention to things such as income taxes and the impact they will have on your net spendable income.

You will want your newfound money to do the best for you in helping meet or exceed your goals and objectives. Don't make the mistake of trying to navigate this trail solo and end up costing yourself unnecessary income taxes or, perhaps worse yet, get yourself in hot water and have to pay penalties and fees on top of taxes because you didn't establish a distribution plan that meets the IRS requirements for distribution.

We have a client that came to us just a short time ago that was set up for taking distributions over a ten-year period from funds that were left to him by his spouse. He received some poor guidance and was told this is how he needed to set up the inherited IRA account. In fact, as the spousal beneficiary he could have established his inherited IRA as an eligible designated beneficiary and spread the income distributions out over his lifetime instead of forcing himself to take much larger distributions today to deplete the account by year 10. This significantly changes his reportable income and forces him into a tax bracket that he could have otherwise avoided with smaller distributions over a longer period.

So, let's see if we can lay a foundation for some basics in terms of retirement plan monies when it comes to beneficiaries.

Beneficiaries of retirement plan and IRA accounts after the death of the account owner are subject to required minimum distribution (RMD) rules. A beneficiary is generally any person or entity the account owner chooses to receive the benefits of a retirement account or an IRA after they die. The owner must designate the beneficiary under procedures established by the plan. Some retirement plans require specific beneficiaries under the terms of the plan (such as a spouse or child).

Beneficiaries of an IRA, and most plans, have the option of taking a lump-sum distribution of the inherited account at any time. Beneficiaries must include any taxable distributions they receive in their gross income.

How beneficiary RMDs are determined

The factors that affect the distribution requirements for inherited retirement plan accounts and IRAs include:

- ◊ Whether the account owner died after 2019 (the SECURE Act made changes to the RMDs for beneficiaries if the death of the account holder occurred after 2019).
- ◊ The relationship of the beneficiary to the account owner and certain characteristics (spouse, minor child, disabled or chronically ill individual, entity other than an individual)
- ◊ Whether the original account owner died before or after their required beginning date (the first date the original account owner was required to begin taking RMDs).

The spouse of the account owner has more options than non-spouse beneficiaries, if they're the sole beneficiary. Determination of whether the spouse is the sole beneficiary is made by September 30 of the year following the year of the account holder's death.

For the year of the account owner's death, the RMD due is the amount the account owner was required to withdraw and did not withdraw before death, if any. Beginning the year following the owner's death, the RMD depends on certain characteristics of the designated beneficiary and the distribution option chosen by the beneficiary.

Death of the account holder occurred before 2020

Spousal beneficiary options

If the death of the account holder occurred prior to the required beginning date, the spousal beneficiary's options are:

◊ Keep as an inherited account
  - Take distributions based on their own life expectancy, or
  - Follow the 5-year rule

◊ Rollover the account into their own IRA

If the death of the account holder occurred after the required beginning date, the spousal beneficiary's options are:

◊ Take distributions based on their own life expectancy
  - No 5-year rule available

Non-spouse beneficiary options

If the account holder's death occurred prior to the required beginning date (or if the account is a Roth IRA), the non-spouse beneficiary's options are:

◊ Take distributions based on their own life expectancy, beginning the end of the year following the year of death, or

◊ Follow the 5-year rule

If the account holder's death occurred after the required beginning date, the non-spouse beneficiary may:

- ◊ Take distributions based on the longer of their own life expectancy or the account owner's remaining life expectancy.

Death of the account holder occurred in 2020 or later

Spousal beneficiary options

If the account holder's death occurred prior to the required beginning date, the spouse beneficiary may:

- ◊ Keep as an inherited account
    - Delay beginning distributions until the employee would have turned 72
    - Take distributions based on their own life expectancy
    - Follow the 10-year rule
- ◊ Roll over the account into their own IRA

If the account holder's death occurred after the required beginning date, the spouse beneficiary may:

- ◊ Keep as an inherited account
    - Take distributions based on their own life expectancy, or
- ◊ Rollover the account into their own IRA

Non-spouse beneficiary options

In 2020 and later, options for a beneficiary who is not the spouse of the deceased account owner depend on whether they are an "eligible designated beneficiary." An eligible designated beneficiary is

- ◊ Spouse or minor child of the deceased account holder

- ◊ Disabled or chronically ill individual
- ◊ Individual who is not more than 10 years younger than the IRA owner or plan participant

An eligible designated beneficiary may

- ◊ Take distributions over the longer of their own life expectancy and the employee's remaining life expectancy, or
- ◊ Follow the 10-year rule (if the account owner died before that owner's required beginning date)

Designated beneficiary (not an eligible designated beneficiary)

- ◊ Follow the 10-year rule

Beneficiary that is not an individual

- ◊ Follow the rules described above as if the account owner died before 2020 (because the SECURE Act changes only apply to beneficiaries who are individuals)

Definitions

5-year rule: If a beneficiary is subject to the 5-year rule,

- ◊ They must empty account by the end of the 5th year following the year of the account holders' death
- ◊ 2020 does not count when determining the 5 years
- ◊ No withdrawals are required before the end of that 5th year

10-year rule: If a beneficiary is subject to the 10-year rule,

- ◊ Empty the entire account by the end of the 10th year following the year of the account owner's (or eligible designated beneficiary's) death

◊ Relief under Notice 2022-53 for beneficiaries subject to the 10-year rule

  - The IRS will not treat a beneficiary of an inherited account in a plan or IRA who was subject to the 10-year rule and who failed to take an RMD for 2021 and 2022 as having failed to take the correct RMD

Eligible designated beneficiary

◊ Spouse or minor child of the deceased account holder

◊ Disabled or chronically ill individual

◊ Individual who is not more than 10 years younger than the IRA owner or plan participant

Designated beneficiary

◊ Any individual designated as the beneficiary of an IRA or retirement plan

Required beginning date

◊ The first date the original account owner was required to begin taking RMDs

Inherited Roth IRAs

Generally, inherited Roth IRA accounts are subject to the same RMD requirements as inherited traditional IRA accounts. Withdrawals of contributions from an inherited Roth are tax free. Most withdrawals of earnings from an inherited Roth IRA account are also tax-free. However, withdrawals of earnings may be subject to income tax if the Roth account is less than 5-years old at the time of the withdrawal.

Distributions from another Roth IRA cannot be substituted for these distributions unless the other Roth IRA was inherited from the same decedent.

Distributions to beneficiaries from qualified retirement plans

If the distribution is from a qualified retirement plan, such as a 401(k) or profit-sharing plan, the plan document establishes the distribution options available to satisfy the RMD rules. The plan administrator should provide the beneficiaries with their distribution options. If the beneficiary is the spouse of the account owner, they may have more distribution options available to them in the plan than a non-spouse beneficiary. Beneficiaries should contact the plan administrator for distributions from a qualified plan.

Income tax on distributions from a retirement plan

Generally, a beneficiary reports pension or annuity income in the same way the plan participant would have reported it. However, some special rules apply.

A beneficiary of an employee who was covered by a retirement plan can exclude from income a portion of nonperiodic distributions received that totally relieve the payer from the obligation to pay an annuity. The amount that the beneficiary can exclude is equal to the deceased employee's investment in the contract (cost).

If the beneficiary is entitled to receive a survivor annuity on the death of an employee, the beneficiary can exclude part of each annuity payment as a tax-free recovery of the employee's investment in the contract. The beneficiary must figure the tax-free part of each payment using the method that applies as if he or she were the employee.

Benefits paid to a survivor under a joint and survivor annuity must be included in the surviving spouse's gross income in the same way the retiree would have included them in gross income.

See, wasn't that easy to follow? Do you feel like you now know what to do if a parent dies and leaves you as their beneficiary of an IRA? Again, we highly recommend speaking to your sherpa if you anticipate receiving funds as a beneficiary and to be sure you have *your own beneficiaries* properly designated on your retirement plan accounts.

What did we learn or confirm here?

1. There are a lot of rules and regulations surrounding Inherited retirement accounts
2. Understanding the rules before taking distributions is very important to avoid penalties
3. In general, non-spouse beneficiaries will have to take receipt of and pay tax on retirement plan monies received over a period not to exceed 10 years

CHAPTER TWELVE

TO ROTH OR NOT TO ROTH, THAT IS THE QUESTION...

As is the case with so many of your planning considerations, finding suitable solutions would be far easier if we all had a crystal ball.

There are two basic scenarios we need to look at here:

1. Whether to be contributing money to pre-tax plans such as traditional IRA accounts and/or pre-tax 401(k) type contributions while you are still accumulating assets for future retirement or to choose a ROTH alternative for these pre-tax plans
2. Whether or not you should convert pre-tax accounts that you had already funded into ROTH accounts in preparation for or during retirement

The tax consequence of the first scenario listed above is going to be spread out over several years and so the tax implication is much smaller each year versus having a larger tax consideration to ponder by converting existing funds into a ROTH plan at a later date. The decision for this latter scenario requires a bit more contemplation in terms of being tax efficient, but it is something we consider with our clients every day and we often use ROTH conversions as part of an overall strategy.

The big overriding question for most people is whether or not future income taxes will be more or less than they are today. This is typically where we run into a disconnect between the level of current income tax rates today and how people *perceive* them to be. Nobody likes paying taxes. The idea that we pay exorbitant levels of income tax today, however, is not based in reality in terms of how we compare to historical rates.

Exhibit 16

2025 Ordinary Income Tax Rates		
Marginal Tax Rates	Married Filing Jointly	Single
10%	$ 0- $23,850	$0- $11,925
12%	$23,851 - $96,950	$11,926 - $48,475
22%	$96,951 - $206,700	$48,476 - $103,351
24%	$206,701 - $394,600	$103,352 - $197,300
32%	$394,601 - $501,050	$197,301 - $250,525
35%	$501,051 - $751,600	$250,526 - $626,350
37%	Over $751,600	Over $626,350

From 1946-1963 the top marginal tax rate was 91% and from 1964-1981 it was 70%. Other than a few short years during more recent times were rates below where they are today.

Here is how you might think about the tax rate question in general: if all else is the same, meaning we use the same assumptions in terms of tax rates and investment returns...the net impact of the overall tax strategy in general will be equal whether or not you do ROTH or Pre-tax. If tax rates increase in the future, you will pay higher tax later than you are saving today. If tax rates are lower in the future, you will have saved the difference.

Now ask yourself whether or not it is more likely we will face higher tax rates down the road based upon what you know about the historical rates and the enormous debt this country is dealing with and a band of politicians who seem unable to balance a checkbook. It is hard not to believe we will be facing higher rates moving forward. And, if you believe we will be facing higher tax rates, go back and ask yourself the question that was posed in a prior chapter...would you rather pay that tax today on the seed you are planting or would you rather pay it on the harvest down the road. We would contend that if rates are going up, pay your tax today on the small seed being planted and avoid income taxes all together when it comes time to harvest the field.

However, there is more to the planning than these simple rules. Being more specific about your plans can really make a difference.

Smart planning can allow you to channel and manage income through lower brackets if they have not been topped out already.

It is also important to consider your specific future income plans when factoring in ROTH conversion options. As an example, we have a current client named Linda who has done a great job saving money for retirement and currently is in her young 50's. She plans to take a few years off work to return to school and therefore will have a significant change in taxable income during this period. She is going to stagger 1/3 of her IRA funds each year over a three-year period, converting her IRA funds to ROTH. She will be doing so in lower brackets than if she were to do this while still earning employment income. Since she will not be accessing these funds for 5 or more years and until she reaches age 59 ½, all future distributions from those funds will be income tax-free.

By spreading the ROTH conversion over three years, Linda and her husband will keep the taxable conversion dollars each year within the 12% tax bracket threshold.

What did we learn or confirm here?

1. Continuously pushing out or deferring taxes will likely lead to paying higher taxes overall than otherwise.
2. Maximizing distributions strategically to force income through lower brackets will likely lead to lower taxes paid overall.
3. Always try and pay tax on income at the lowest rate possible. (this means don't waste lower bracket thresholds)
4. Pre-tax savings plans such as IRA's are less favorable than they were prior to the Secure Act, particularly as they pertain to funds being left to a non-spouse beneficiary.

CHAPTER THIRTEEN

ANNUITIES

An annuity is a financial product that provides a series of payments to an individual at regular intervals, usually after retirement. It is primarily used to secure a steady income stream and manage longevity risk by converting savings into periodic payments over time. (Certainty)

In our world, there is a lot of confusion about annuities, however, and it starts with the definition above. While the definition may technically be correct, meaning it relates to a periodic stream of income, we use annuities in many different ways today and often they are used as an accumulation tool with features that include establishing a periodic income stream, but the corresponding features of tax deferral and guaranteed principal protection tend to be bigger reasons for using them in an overall plan.

Inherent in the types of annuities listed below, each of them may be established in one of two ways:

◊ **Immediate Annuities**: These start payments almost immediately after a lump sum is invested, providing instant income, ideal for retirees who need income right away.

◊ **Deferred Annuities**: Payments begin at a future date, allowing the investment to grow tax-deferred until distributions begin, used by those who want to maximize growth before retirement.

Types of Annuities

The variation in the three main categories of Annuity Products noted below; Fixed, Variable, Indexed is the underlying way your money is invested/allocated. Fixed Annuities offer guaranteed fixed rates of return, variable annuities include separate account funds that provide exposure to equity and bond investments and indexed annuities are somewhat of a hybrid of the other two by providing access to a fixed guaranteed rate account as well as providing access to market related returns through allocations that track various indexes such as the S&P 500. The advantage to the indexed annuity is that your principal and any earnings are protected against loss from market returns, providing an opportunity for growth far beyond that of a fixed rate annuity, but without all the risk associated with a variable annuity.

1. Fixed Annuities: These provide guaranteed payments at a fixed rate, often suitable for conservative investors. They offer security and predictability, making them popular among retirees seeking stable income.

2. Variable Annuities: The payouts vary based on the performance of underlying investments, like stocks or bonds. These are chosen by retirees who are comfortable with market risk and seek higher potential returns. Variable annuities tend to be expensive in terms of fees and charges and should be considered carefully. We do not currently offer variable annuities in our planning.

3. Indexed Annuities: These are tied to a stock or bond index, offering returns based partially on market performance, with some protection against loss, balancing growth and security.

Since annuities seem to get a fair amount of airtime and often that airtime is spent telling you all the things that are wrong about annuities, we think it is important for you to understand that you will absolutely do yourself a disservice to get caught up in that propaganda without knowing exactly what it is that is being discussed. We would also point out here, as is the case with virtually everything in life, you have to understand the source of your information.

There are companies that have published entire books trying to dissuade people from using annuities in their retirement planning considerations. It is easy to see, however, the goal is to dissuade you from using something they do not offer, not because they don't serve a purpose, but because purchasing one does not fit their business model for getting paid fees on assets under management in an investment portfolio. So, we often see, as is the case in the book we are referencing, annuities described as inefficient and including lots of fees and costs, portraying them in the worst of light and in complete contrast to how we might use them and design them to meet a client's specific goals and objectives.

We use annuities often in our planning with clients…and we do so for a variety of reasons in terms of meeting specific client goals. We purposely look to avoid policies with fees and expenses that erode the annual returns being sought and we always *consider* annuities when we are attempting to provide principal protection on specific assets, coupled with an opportunity for growth, followed by a period where income will be distributed.

Imagine if someone came up to you tomorrow and described the following option for you as part of your overall retirement strategy;

1. 100% Principal Guarantee-this means you cannot lose money based upon losses from any investment allocation within the plan.
2. When you do earn money, that too becomes part of your principal and is no longer subject to risk.
3. All earnings are tax-deferred until you start to take money out. (This means you avoid taxes until you use the money)
4. No fees or charges assuming you follow the plan as designed.
5. You have an opportunity to earn market related returns without actually being in the market and therefore avoiding the risk of investment loss or negative returns.
6. You can choose to allocate your monies in a fixed guaranteed account, split it among a vast array of index allocations or do a combination of both fixed and indexed and you can change these selections periodically according to terms you will know in advance, and which cannot be changed by the company issuing the program.
7. You can name a beneficiary or beneficiaries and avoid money having to pass through probate at your death.
8. You can fund this with money that has either already been taxed or with money that has never been taxed such as IRA assets, rollovers from your 401(k) or similar employer sponsored retirement plan, etc. And in some cases, you can auto-

matically convert pre-tax dollars to after-tax dollars without losing any of the other benefits of the plan.

9. You will have a number of options as to how you want to take the money out when the time comes; you can simply withdraw a portion of your account and leave the remaining balance as it was prior to withdrawal, you can establish a lifetime income stream that you cannot outlive or in some cases you may have options that include joint lifetime incomes to both you and your spouse with a strong opportunity for that income to increase each year over time.

It is hard for us to imagine that the partial list of attributes and features noted above wouldn't at least inspire you to consider such an option as part of an overall retirement planning strategy. There are no other places in the world where you can have access to market-related returns without the risk associated with the market. When you add attributes such as 100% principal and earnings protection as well as efficient transfer at death, you begin to realize there might be a place in your diversified plan for such a program.

Please remember that it is far more important to understand what plans can do for you in terms of your goals and objectives than it is what something is called. So, don't let the word annuity scare you. Judge things on what they can do for you, not what they are called. And be vigilant about understanding what it is you are looking at when considering various choices for your money.

If you remember some of the risks listed in prior chapters, you quickly see how one program can help mitigate many, many risks associated with the choices you have for your money at retirement time.

◊ **Interest Rate Risk**-interest rate risk is the risk of being too conservative with your investments in a way that you far underperform opportunity and do not keep pace with inflation. This happens when people are afraid of market volatility and seek shelter from risk…often choosing plans that provide security but not enough upside potential to meet their goals and objectives. Indexed Annuities provide the shelter some people are seeking without taking away the upside earnings potential and therefore avoiding interest rate risk.

◊ **Market Volatility-** other than variable annuities, which we do not offer, market volatility is minimized in that you cannot lose money based upon market performance in a no-fee fixed or indexed annuity.

◊ **Negative Sequence of Return-**you cannot have a negative sequence of return in something that provides guaranteed principal protection. Negative sequence occurs when market returns are negative. That can't happen in a fixed or indexed annuity. At the very worst, in an indexed annuity, if your allocation choices do not perform well and index returns are negative, your contract will receive no less than a zero return for that period. We like to say in these instances, "Zero is your Hero".

◊ **Long Term Chronic Illness-**there are annuity products built specifically to help secure against a long-term chronic illness event where you might be subjected to exorbitant costs as discussed in the chapter on Long Term Care.

Annuities for Long-Term Care

(See Chapter 5 for more in-depth discussion on this topic)

A **Hybrid Annuity/Long-Term Care policy** combines features of an annuity with long-term care insurance. These policies use a portion of the annuity to pay for long-term care expenses if needed.

How It Works:

◊ **Investment and Growth**: You invest a sum, which grows over time.

◊ **Long-Term Care Coverage**: If long-term care is needed, the policy provides tax-free benefits to cover care costs.

◊ **Flexibility**: If not used for care, the annuity can still provide retirement income or pass to beneficiaries.

Hybrid annuities offer retirees financial security by ensuring funds are available for long-term care while still providing a reliable income stream during retirement. This dual protection supports both regular retirement needs and potential long-term care expenses, offering a comprehensive financial planning tool.

In summary, annuities come in a million different flavors and should not be viewed with a broad brush. They are often excellent tools for providing specific features or benefits that can provide predictability, security and certainty in terms of investment return, asset accumulation and/or guaranteed income. The exact features and specific objectives being offered in any one of the many options out there today is what is key. Design and choice will define your plan in a way that allows you to build something in an annuity product that can accomplish many different objectives at little to no cost and perhaps provide a baseline of guarantees that will allow you to approach your non-annuity assets in a different way. As an example, if you have your basic needs covered for the foreseeable future through a guaranteed solution, you will be free to be more aggressive in your investment strategy on your portfolio of market related assets such as stocks and bonds. The overall results may help you earn greater returns overall and outpace inflation while also knowing you have covered your bases should the market results be less than you anticipated.

We have spoken about safe money rates and the idea that if you try and take too much income from your assets you run the risk of depleting your nest egg before you have met your demise. By providing downside protection with a 0% floor, eliminating the risk of market-related losses, you can withdraw more money from your funds each year without increasing the risk of running out of money. In many cases, this is the only option for us in planning to help someone meet their needs. If a higher safe distribution rate is needed, a solution that provides downside protection while also providing an opportunity for growth above what a fixed account rate will provide is really the only way to get the job done.

What did we learn or confirm here?

1. Annuities come in a million flavors and do not all work the same
2. Choosing the right annuity and designing it with the right features and benefits is the key to having success with an annuity
3. Fixed and Fixed -Indexed Annuities provide principal guarantees to protect your funds from market fluctuations-this in-

cludes both the funds you put into the annuity as well as the earnings it makes while invested

4. Principal protection can change the dynamic of calculating a safe money distribution rate, ideally leading to the opportunity to withdraw money at a higher rate than you can from a managed portfolio

5. Fixed and Indexed Annuities can be used as multi-tasking financial vehicles protecting assets from an investment point of view as well as helping assure additional funds are available in the event of a long-term chronic illness

CHAPTER FOURTEEN

MODERN DAY LIFE INSURANCE

We really should have named this chapter similarly to what we did regarding pension plans. As in, Not your Grandad's Life Insurance. We have seen the life insurance industry adapt and change to meet consumer needs perhaps more than any other segment of the financial markets. The policies offered today include benefits and features that were unheard of when your granddad was considering life insurance for his family. In particular, the addition of *"living benefits"* has provided a reason to look at life insurance even more so for *what it does, not what it is.*

Life insurance provides financial protection and peace of mind to policyholders and their beneficiaries. Here's a brief overview of the benefits and types of life insurance:

Benefits of Life Insurance

1. Financial Security: Provides a death benefit to beneficiaries, ensuring financial support after the policyholder's death.

2. Debt Coverage: Helps cover outstanding debts, such as mortgages and loans.
3. Income Replacement: Replaces lost income for dependents, maintaining their standard of living.
4. Estate Planning: Supports estate planning strategies and can assist in covering estate taxes.
5. Living Benefits: Some policies offer the ability to access funds during the policyholder's life.
6. Wealth Transfer: Leveraging discretionary retirement funds to create income tax free benefits

Types of Life Insurance

1. **Term Life Insurance:**
   - ◊ **What it is**: Provides coverage for a specific term (e.g., 10, 20, 30 years).
   - ◊ **Solution Provided**: Affordable and straightforward, ideal for temporary needs such as income replacement during working years.
2. **Whole Life Insurance:**
   - ◊ **What it is**: Permanent coverage with fixed premiums and cash value accumulation.
   - ◊ **Solution Provided**: Offers lifelong protection and can be used as a savings or investment vehicle.
3. **Universal Life Insurance:**
   - ◊ **What it is**: Permanent insurance with flexible premiums and adjustable death benefits.

◊ **Solution Provided**: Combines life insurance with investment options, allowing policyholders greater control over premiums and benefits.

4. **Variable Life Insurance:**

◊ **What it is**: Permanent insurance with investment options within separate accounts.

◊ **Solution Provided**: Allows policyholders to invest in various accounts, potentially increasing the policy's cash value.

Living Benefits

Life insurance today can be utilized as a living benefit through accelerated death benefits. This feature allows the policyholder to access a portion of the death benefit while still alive, typically in cases of terminal illness, critical illness, or confinement to a nursing home. This provides financial help to cover medical expenses, improve quality of life, or support other personal needs.

Overall, life insurance not only provides traditional death benefits but also offers versatile solutions tailored to various financial goals and stages of life.

CHAPTER FIFTEEN

ESTATE PLANNING 101

Whether or not you have a substantive estate and regardless of your family and business situation, there are some basic estate planning tools that should benefit everyone with their estate disposition objectives. Failing to avail yourself with these tools will likely lead to significant delays in disposing of your assets at the time of your death, may result in far less *net* assets passing to heirs and potentially creating significant discontent among family and other heirs for which you likely desired a smooth and uneventful transfer of your wealth.

Considerations for maintaining a current Estate Plan

There are lots of life events that can demand changes to your estate planning directives. Make sure to keep a list like this handy so you recognize when attention is needed to your plans.

◊ Changes in investment and tax laws-particularly estate tax laws

◊ Marital Status Changes

◊ Changes in property ownership

- ◊ The receipt of large sums from inheritance or by gift
- ◊ Birth and/or adoption of new children or grandchildren
- ◊ Minors reaching age of majority
- ◊ Major changes in financial objectives
- ◊ Family experiencing death, disability or other illness
- ◊ Changes to life insurance or long-term care policies
- ◊ Significant changes in your balance sheet-what you own and what you owe
- ◊ Changes in who will manage your estate /affairs
- ◊ Career changes, including promotions, new jobs, or starting or closing a business

Basics of Estate Planning

Even a basic estate plan should include the following important items to try and avoid unwanted outcomes

- ◊ **WILLS and TRUSTS** - A Will is a legal document that outlines how your assets will be distributed after your death. It allows you to name beneficiaries for your property, designate guardians for minor children, and appoint an executor to carry out your wishes. A Trust, on the other hand, is a legal entity created to hold and manage assets during your lifetime and after your death.
- ◊ **Beneficiary designations-** Beneficiary designations refer to the individuals or entities you name to receive specific assets upon your death.

- ◊ **Durable power of attorney** - A durable Power of Attorney is a legal document that grants someone you trust the authority to manage your financial and legal affairs if you become incapacitated.
- ◊ **Guardianship designations** - Name a person or persons who will take legal responsibility for your minor children if both parents pass away or are otherwise unable to care for them.
- ◊ **Healthcare power of attorney** - A healthcare Power of Attorney (also known as a medical power of attorney) is a legal document that allows you to appoint someone to make medical decisions on your behalf if you cannot do so.

Here is a checklist to get you started as you begin to arrange for the creation of a viable estate plan.

1. Assets (What you own)

Make a list of all tangible and intangible assets.

Sample Tangible Assets to record

- ◊ Personal possessions (jewelry, electronics)
- ◊ Real estate, both residential and investment related
- ◊ Vehicles (cars, bikes, boats)
- ◊ Collectibles (art, coins)

Sample Intangible Assets to record

- ◊ Life insurance policies
- ◊ Bank accounts and CDs

- ◊ Retirement Accounts
- ◊ Health savings accounts
- ◊ Non-retirement investment accounts with investment accounts
- ◊ Business ownership

Keep track of the value of these assets and be sure to record and make available account numbers and physical documents that may be needed upon your death. Remember to include contact information for the companies and individuals that are managing these accounts.

Side note: Don't forget to include technology-based info that would be helpful to whomever is managing your affairs after your death. Passwords and a list of social media accounts will likely save someone a lot of unnecessary research time.

2. Liabilities (What you owe)

Create a comprehensive list of all debt obligations, including:

- ◊ Residential and commercial mortgages
- ◊ Lines of credit
- ◊ Car, truck and equipment loans
- ◊ Credit cards
- ◊ Other debts

3. Memberships

Document membership so you can provide additional benefits and information for your beneficiaries and list organizations such as

◊ Veterans associations

◊ Professional associations

◊ Alumni groups

Be sure to include any life insurance or other survivor benefits and tell your beneficiaries which charities you support.

4. **Retirement and Insurance Accounts**

Be sure your desired beneficiaries are properly listed and with up-to-date contact information, take advantage of naming contingent beneficiaries whenever you can and try not to leave beneficiary designations unnamed.

Remember, particularly with things like retirement accounts, your beneficiary designation may result in substantive tax consequences. Failure to take care here can mean your assets not only might pass to an unintended party, but the tax consequences of doing so may significantly diminish the value of your asset. We recommend you consult with your sherpa to be sure you understand the impact of having the right person or entity receiving your bequest.

5. Evaluate Family / Survivor Needs

Protect your assets and the best interests of your beneficiaries by regular evaluation of items that can directly and immediately impact their livelihood when you are gone.

◊ Is your life insurance adequate to fill gaps left behind in your financial plan

◊ How will your survivors manage your assets to best meet their needs

◊ Are there things you can do today to eliminate uncertainty for your survivors in the future

6. Transfer on Death (TOD) Designations

Leaving your checking account to your loved one by way of your Last Will and Testament does not mean that same loved one can begin using the checking account the day you die. Assets passing by way of your Will still need to be probated and access to these accounts, until the probate court allows, may be significantly delayed and cause undue financial stress on survivors. You should consider establishing TOD designations for brokerage, CD, and bank accounts to avoid probate. You can contact your bank or custodian to properly set up TOD designations on your accounts, leaving these accounts available to your intended recipients with the least amount of potential delay.

7. Digital Assets

Digital assets play a bigger and bigger part in today's estate planning considerations. Don't leave your beneficiaries or executors hanging -have a record of all things digital

◊ Email account names, passwords

◊ Social media account names and passwords

◊ Website domain names and passwords

You should include your login information and ensure that beneficiaries have legal consent in your Will and Power of Attorney to access digital information.

8. Use Legal Directives

Choose a responsible estate executor, be clear in your intentions and directives and use legal tools as noted below to best assure your wishes are defined and able to be met upon your demise

- ◊ Trusts (Revocable and Irrevocable)
- ◊ Medical care directives (advance health care directives)
- ◊ Durable financial power of attorney
- ◊ Limited power of attorney

Assign appropriate people to handle different issues such as financial and medical representation. As with your beneficiary designations, try and have contingency plans already built into your plan in case a named executor or other representative cannot serve your needs as your first choice when establishing the original plan.

9. Professional Oversight

Just as it is important to have a financial sherpa helping you navigate the route to and from the summit, so too is it important that a professional help you design and implement a plan for when you ultimately reach base camp.

Consider hiring an experienced estate planning lawyer who can work together with your financial sherpa to best navigate this important process. We have trusted and competent local relationships in this regard and will gladly help facilitate an introduction if you need one.

10. Follow through on required documents

Completing the task of creating and using your estate plan requires that you follow through with your plans. We can't tell you how many times people take time to plan and visit with an estate planning professional only to fall short in putting the documents needed into place and/or also failing to make necessary changes in asset ownership, etc that are needed to be made for your plan to work properly. Your documents are likely to include the following as a minimum

- ◊ Last Will and Testament
- ◊ Health care proxy
- ◊ Durable power of attorney
- ◊ Living will
- ◊ Guardianship for minor children and pets

What did we learn or confirm here?

1. There are several basic estate planning tools that apply to virtually everyone, whether you have significant wealth or not
2. Estate Planning should not be driven solely for tax efficiency
3. Proper estate planning, even on a basic level can help provide tax efficiency, but also ensure that assets are distributed according to your wishes with little to nothing being left to the direction of a probate court

4. As things change it is important to keep your estate plan up to date-we recommend an annual review

CHAPTER SIXTEEN

NAVIGATING THE ROAD AHEAD

So, here we are...by now we hope that you have taken note that there are many things that you need to consider when planning for your journey ahead. We thought it would make sense to review in summary fashion some of the more important things for you to remember as you get your rucksack loaded up.

Our most important concept to grasp in terms of good long-term planning is that while you should and must find ways to maximize your overall return on your money, achieving the highest rate of return does not automatically result in mitigating risks that could derail your entire journey.

Additionally, there is value in certainty and by incorporating some guaranteed elements to your overall planning you can manage and mitigate risks without sacrificing your ability to enjoy your retirement and provide yourself with valuable "peace of mind".

Our intention in writing this book was to be sure we highlighted what we feel are many of the most important things for you to know or learn as you approach and move past the Summit.

We hope that if nothing else, you grasp the notion that the distribution phase of your financial life is very different than the accumulation phase of your financial life and you should find significant value in meeting with professionals who have experience in dealing with this planning process.

Key Highlights

Managing risk is *as* important, if not more important, in retirement income planning than achieving the highest rate of return

Managing risk can provide more certainty to your plans and changes how you think about and use your retirement plan assets and can lead to more probable success with your journey

There are several ways to manage various risks including asset repositioning, use of market volatility buffers, and utilizing actuarial based products with underlying guarantees

The assumptions used in modeling income plans are the devil in the details. Flawed assumptions lead to flawed results

The retirement planning road is littered with potholes and other hazards, and you will likely fair best by having a financial sherpa along for the trip

The best time to begin planning is NOW. As our retired Marine Corp Captain, David Kutcher, likes to say, "*No Delay!*"

We look forward to working with you and helping you incorporate a plan providing for *"Safety, Growth and Control"*

CHAPTER SEVENTEEN

WAIT, THERE'S MORE!!

Wouldn't you know it? No sooner were we on our way to publishing when the "One Big Beautiful Bill Act of 2025" (OBBBA 2025) hit the streets.

We would be remiss not to add this chapter at this time so please note some changes that have come about under the OBBBA 2025.

Summary:

1. There are NO changes directly related to retirement plan contribution limits or ROTH contribution rules. Some provisions in the OBBBA 2025 may indirectly, however, require some consideration for your own plans
2. STANDARD Deduction INCREASE: $15,750 single and $31,500 married filing jointly are the new 2025 amounts, and these will be indexed based upon CPI moving forward.
3. EXTRA SENIOR DEDUCTION: Additional $6,000 standard deduction over the next three years for taxpayers age 65 +. (2025-2028) Additional deduction applies whether or not itemizing deductions. Additional deductions applies whether

or not receiving the extra deduction already for aged 65 or blind.

◊ The additional deduction phases out at higher income limits; starting at $75,000 for single taxpayers and $150,000 for those married and filing jointly.

◊ Phase out of additional deduction is complete at $175,000 and $250,000 respectively.

◊ Maximum total deduction under this provision for a married couple filing jointly is a whopping $45,700 when adding all components of this together.

◊ Please note this deduction is below the Adjusted Gross Income line in your taxes which means it does not lower your income for items such as determining whether or not your social security benefits are taxable.

◊ Taxpayers who are involved in ROTH conversions should take care that conversions are taxable income events that can move the needle on whether you reach the phase out limits mentioned above.

4. ESTATE and GIFT TAXES: Federal Estate and Gift tax exclusions are $15,000,000 for individuals and $30,000,000 for couples. These limits will also be CPI indexed moving forward.

5. FEDERAL INCOME TAX RATES: The reduction of the income tax rates that we were currently enjoying from the 2017 Tax Cuts and Jobs Act and was due to expire this year are extended permanently…or at least as permanent as we can get. Please refer back to Exhibit 16 for current rate thresholds.

6. TIPS: For the years 2025-2028 there is a tax deduction for up to $25,000 of tip income applying to either a single or married taxpayer. The deduction phases out at higher income amounts; $150,000 for single and $300,000 for married filing jointly.

7. OVERTIME: For the years 2025-2028 there is a tax deduction for up to $12,500 of overtime pay for single taxpayers and $25,000 for married filing jointly. The deduction phases out at higher income amounts; $150,000 for single and $300,000 for married filing jointly.

8. REDUCTION of ITEMIZED Deductions for top tax bracket. Anyone subject to the 37% top bracket who itemizes deductions will receive the deduction at the 35% bracket... meaning the deduction percentage is lower than the actual tax bracket and maxes out at 35% rate. This is effective in 2026.

9. CHARITABLE DEDUCTIONS: For people who do NOT itemize but make charitable contributions, you can deduct up to $1,000 as single taxpayer, $2,000 for married couples filing jointly. This deduction is reduced by .5% of adjusted gross income.

10. CHILD TAX CREDIT: Effective 2025 the child tax credit permanently increases to $2,200 per child and will be adjusted for CPI moving forward. No change in income limits for this credit from prior years.

STATE and LOCAL TAX DEDUCTIONS for those Itemizing deductions: The State and Local tax deduction is increased to $40,000 for each individual. This is one of the few items where there is a marriage penalty as two single taxpayers can each use their $40,000 deduction if their income limits do not phase them out, whereas a married couple fling jointly is limited to the same $40,000. Phase out begins at $500,000 of income for single and married filing jointly and is completely phased out by $600,000. There is a $10,000 deduction remaining at the $600,000 income level. This means a taxpayer at $600,000 plus of income will be limited to the $10,000 deduction rather than the base $40,000 deduction available to those making less income.

◊ With the higher deduction limits, planning can facilitate more tax efficient ROTH conversion considerations. If you can combine deductions under the higher deduction limits in years where you may consider converting pre-tax dollars to ROTH accounts, the higher deduction limits for 2025-2029 may provide some reprieve from income taxes that come due at time of ROTH conversions.

11. TRUMP BABY Accounts: effective July 2026 contributions can be made on behalf of a child up to $5,000 per year and babies born between January 1, 2025 and December 31, 2028 will be started with a $1,000 contribution by the government.

◊ Baby accounts are considered and treated as IRA until child reaches age 18

◊ No compensation requirements to make contributions

◊ Contributions do NOT count against other IRA or retirement plan limits

◊ Money must be invested in low cost mutual funds or ETF of US stock index such as the S&P 500 index

◊ May be eligible for ROTH at age 18

◊ Funds cannot be withdrawn before age 18 years of age

There are some other provisions related to business owners in the OBBBA 2025 that go beyond the scope of this chapter. If you are self-employed, feel free to reach out to us to discuss how the new rules may impact decisions you make in terms of your Qualified Business Income Deduction. Particularly if you are considering ROTH conversions…this is an area that will require some attention, so you don't phase yourself out or otherwise inadvertently add to the ROTH conversion taxes or impact your limits negatively in terms of being able to take the 20% Qualified Business Income Deduction.

What did we learn or confirm here?

1. OBBBA 2025 includes permanent cuts and should help with considering future planning under today's assumptions

2. While inflation is not seen as having a positive impact on retirement income efficiency, any CPI adjustments to current tax bracket thresholds expand the threshold amounts and will allow for more money to flow through lower tax brackets than if the brackets were not indexed for inflation

3. ROTH conversion considerations are extended under historically low income-tax rates. There is no time like the present to consider ROTH conversion as part of your retirement income planning strategy

One final note…we are not accountants, and any tax information contained herein is intended to be a summary presentation as we interpret it from the IRS. You should always seek formal tax advice from a tax professional such as a CPA. We work side by side with you and your other professional advisors, particularly in legal and tax planning considerations.

Thank you!!

www.ingramcontent.com/pod-product-compliance
Lightning Source LLC
LaVergne TN
LVHW070826220926
848486LV00027B/28